HAUNTED DELAND AND THE GHOSTS OF WEST VOLUSIA COUNTY

HAUNTED DELAND AND THE GHOSTS OF WEST VOLUSIA COUNTY

DUSTY SMITH

Haunted America

Published by Haunted America
A Division of The History Press
Charleston, SC 29403
www.historypress.net

First published 2008

Manufactured in the United States

ISBN 978.1.59629.526.1

Library of Congress Cataloging-in-Publication Data

Smith, Doris (Doris "Dusty")
Haunted Deland : the ghosts of West Volusia County / Dusty Smith.
p. cm.
Includes bibliographical references.
ISBN 978-1-59629-526-1
1. Ghosts--Florida--De Land. 2. Haunted places--Florida--De Land. I. Title.
BF1472.U6S595 2008
133.109759'21--dc22
2008028568

Notice: The information in this book is true and complete to the best of our knowledge. It is offered without guarantee on the part of the author or The History Press. The author and The History Press disclaim all liability in connection with the use of this book.

For the hard work and dedication of all of the members of the West Volusia Historical Society, Bill Dreggors, Harry W. Wise, Opal Lee, the City of DeLand, the staff of the Cassadaga Hotel and the people of the towns of DeLand, Cassadaga and Lake Helen for making the information available to make this book a possibility.

Without people like you, our history would fade away into the black void and our children wouldn't know where they come from. It is very important for all of us to continue to preserve history in any way we can so as not to forget what we have done, so we can learn from our mistakes and make this world a better place for our children's children to exist in.

I applaud and thank each and every one of you for your tireless and thankless efforts, no matter how large or small.

Contents

Acknowledgements

I would like to dedicate this work to the following people:

To my son Kyle: Kyle has been my inspiration for many years, at times my muse and always my hero. I am more proud of him than words can state. He is a good human being, with a kind heart, a brilliant mind and more compassion and empathy for others than anyone else I know. He has helped me over the years with my research, my cemetery preservation efforts, my strange collections, my ghost tours, my writing, my attempts to learn to use computers and other technical gadgets, any and all new projects that come my way and by always being there when I need a friend. He is now a wonderful young man that has left the nest and has broken my heart by doing so. However, I understand his need to be on his own, and I am very proud of him for making the right decisions in his now-adult life. I miss him being at home every night but appreciate him stopping by once a week to eat dinner and watch a movie with his crazy mom while he does his laundry. I love you Kyle and I am proud to be your mother.

To my good friend Harry W. Wise aka "Wise the Wizard": Harry came into my life through a mutual friend and has never left. We enjoy long phone calls together and eating out at Hampton's restaurant when we can. He has taught me about stage magic and old movies and I have taught him about cemetery preservation and Living Dead Dolls. Harry is a brilliant man who at one time was a very famous stage magician, performing a "ghost show" all over the United States. He is now retired and misses being center stage—I empathize with him. He has been a great friend and a good confidant and he always makes me laugh. Thank you Harry for your contributions to this world and to this book.

To Tom Begley: May you rest in peace until we meet again in the next life. Stick around a little longer next time please.

To Doug Kelley: Thank you for being a great friend, awesome fellow researcher and wonderful and patient Webmaster.

To all of the following people: Kathleen the Elder VanHozza, Steve Williams, Bill Sharpe, Troy Taylor, Jason Hawes, Grant Wilson, Patrick and Pamela Burns, Bill Bean, the Wyricks, Deborah Collard, Dr. Ed Craft, Karen Harvey, Dave Juliano, Dave Schrader, Dr. William Roll, Hans Holzer, Bill Metz, Don Graham, Dan Asfar, Jeff Belanger, Steve Gonsalves, the Ghost Chics, Dr. Alan Brown, Brad Steiger, Jeffrey Breslauer, Tiffany Johnson, Keith Age, Joey Ward, Denise Rolf, John J. Oliver, Tim Yancey, Bob Hunnicut, Michael and Marti Parry, Reese Christian, Bill Chappel, Midnight Syndicate, Elvira and the rest of the paranormal, horror and cemetery communities who have given me the motivation to continue in these fields. You are all my friends and I appreciate everything you have done for and with me over the years.

To Frank Perrick: Thank you for spending the day with me and driving me all over creation to get some of the photos for this book. You are a true friend and I will always love you just the way you are—don't ever change for anyone except you!

Introduction

Hundreds of thousands of people all over the world find the subject of ghosts fascinating. I have been conducting paranormal investigations and ghost hunting for nearly fifteen years now, and I meet many people from all walks of life that all have their own personal stories to tell. Most remember something strange from when they were a child, some still live in a home that has odd occurrences and still others have such a passion for this subject that they never seem to get enough of it.

With the resurgence in the field of the paranormal, many of these people seek out as much information on the subjects as they can find. With the many television shows, conferences, groups, ghost tours and books available these days, it has become an industry unto itself. What some people may not realize about this field is that there is a great deal of history involved in "creating" a ghost. Our history forms who we are as living people as well as holds the spirits of the dead to given locations. A great example is Gettysburg.

Since so many people lost their lives in a very short time and under great emotional pressure during the battles fought at Gettysburg, those facts make it one of the most haunted locations in the United States. But there are so many other places in the country that also hold emotional energy from times gone—energy that keeps spirits active today. There didn't have to be a battle, war, plague, famine or other major tragedy, although those types of things do help in the creation of a haunting. Looking into the background of a given location can sometimes give us clues as to why a haunting may be taking place.

While history was not a favorite subject of mine growing up, it has become an integral part of my adult life. Many of the private cases that the Daytona Beach Paranormal Research Group, Inc. has worked on over the past thirteen years can be directly linked to events that have taken place on the land hundreds and sometimes thousands of years ago. People think that this work is a lot of fun—and don't get me wrong, it can be—but most of what ghost hunters and paranormal investigators do is boring!

First things first. The difference between a ghost hunter and a paranormal investigator is that ghost hunters search for ghosts in areas known to be haunted, while paranormal investigators study locations where paranormal activity has been reported. Those two things may sound the same, but believe me, they are very different. A good example would be that a ghost hunter goes into an old building for which there have been numerous reports of apparitions and colds spots over the years. They set up their equipment, take photos, record audio and after a couple of hours go over the documentation they acquired. A paranormal investigator receives a call from a family member that claims to have heard strange noises in the middle of the night and experienced cold spots and object movement. The paranormal investigator interviews the witnesses, maps the location, does a historical background check of the area, sets up equipment similar to that of the ghost hunter and tries to find manmade or naturally occurring reasons for the purported activity before stating that the location is haunted. Any evidence collected during their several hours spent on site is gone over with a fine-toothed comb and later presented to the client to show the reasons why—or why not—the area is actually haunted.

With all of that stated, you also need to know what types of hauntings you may run across in whichever field you decide to venture into, if any. Knowledge is the key to understanding and overcoming our fears. There are four basic types of hauntings. One is called an intelligent haunting. This type of haunting is associated with the spirit of a once-living human being that doesn't realize they have passed on, for whatever reason—they died suddenly, as in a murder or car accident, or maybe they were very old and wanted to live even longer. It is also possible that they chose to remain behind. I know that if I passed away and my son was still young and I was given the choice of whether I would stay behind and keep an eye on whoever was taking care of him or to cross over to the other side—I would choose to remain behind. No one is quit sure why spirits of this type are here, but they are called intelligent hauntings because they retain their intellect, personality and emotions and still interact with their surroundings. They participate in the physical world as they did when they were still alive.

The second type of haunting is known as a poltergeist haunting. This type of haunting comes from a German word that means "knocking," "banging" or "noisy" ghost. This type of haunting is often confused with an intelligent haunting because the spirit does tend to interact with its surroundings. The difference is that a poltergeist is very mischievous. They like to hide your car keys, tug your hair, bang on walls or doors, ring the door bell—object movement is very pronounced when a poltergeist spirit is present in a location. Poltergeist activity can also be created by the living. Psychokinetic energy created in the human brain from hormonal activity can cause poltergeist activity. Science has shown that in pre- and postpubescent teenage males and females, pre- and postmenopausal women and even pregnant women, poltergeist activity can be directly related to that person in the home. If none of the types of people who fall into any of those categories are present in the area of paranormal activity, then you can pretty much lay money on the fact that you have a true poltergeist haunting.

The third type of haunting is known as a demonic haunting. This type of haunting is pretty self-explanatory. A demon or demonic entity takes up residence in an area, usually a home, and sets out to tear the family apart emotionally, psychologically and physically. This type of haunting, while severe, is also very rare.

The fourth and most common type of haunting is known as a residual or residue haunting. This type of haunting occurs because of a very strong emotional event that takes place when someone is alive and the atmospheric conditions are prime—the energy from that event literally imprints onto space and time and then plays over and over like a time-loop film would. A good example would consist of a young woman who was deeply in love with a man who died suddenly. She visits his grave, grieving for decades after. The emotional energy she is exuding into the atmosphere is imprinting onto space and time and her form begins to be seen by others. Sometimes the residual energy is so strong that the person doesn't even need to have died yet for the haunting to occur. Most often, though, the person has passed away. The person's soul or spirit is no longer attached—it is only the event playing over and over for all eternity.

Now that you are armed with all the necessary information to begin this journey, you will find that while DeLand is a small, historic, sleepy town in central Florida, its many past and present residents are deeply devoted to life there. So many people have lived, loved and died in DeLand that its spirit activity rivals that of many other larger, more well-known, areas of ghostly activity.

Unlike my book *Haunted Daytona Beach: A Ghostly Tour of the World's Most Famous Beach*, not all of the stories in this book have been documented as true hauntings. While several of them have been, some of these stories are just good old-fashioned ghost stories. I do mention in some of the stories which ones have been documented; however, with the information you just read about how ghosts are "created," see if you can figure out which stories are true hauntings and which are just plain stories, and what kind of hauntings they are.

If you're ever lucky enough to visit the DeLand area, be sure to stop by some of these locations and see if you have any luck finding the ghosts of DeLand.

Chapter 1

The Spirits of Stetson University

The city of DeLand was named after its founder, Henry A. DeLand. DeLand was a retired baking powder manufacturer from Fairport, New York. He came to Florida in 1876 and purchased a large tract of land and began to lay out plans for the city that at the time he called Spring Hill. Little by little, settlers arrived, opened stores, built homes and planted orange groves. People began calling the community DeLand, and in 1882, voters decided to make the name of the city official and incorporated it into what is now known as the city of DeLand.

Two years later, Henry DeLand and another New Yorker, Berlin Wright, decided to develop a small resort town on the shores of a lake between DeLand and the Spiritualist camp town known as Cassadaga. They called both the body of water and the community Lake Helen, after Henry's daughter Helen.

Like many advertisers pitching a project, DeLand promised a money-back guarantee to anyone who bought citrus land from him and was dissatisfied. Unlike many other advertisers, DeLand kept his promise. When a freeze struck the area's citrus crop in January of 1886, DeLand was faced with dozens of dissatisfied investors who wanted their money back. Keeping his word financially ruined him, but DeLand paid back the investors and then had to return to New York and his baking powder business.

One person attracted to the area by Henry DeLand's advertisements was John B. Stetson, the billionaire hat manufacturer. He arrived in 1886, shortly after the freeze. He couldn't have come at a better time as far as the city's future was concerned. When the freeze wiped

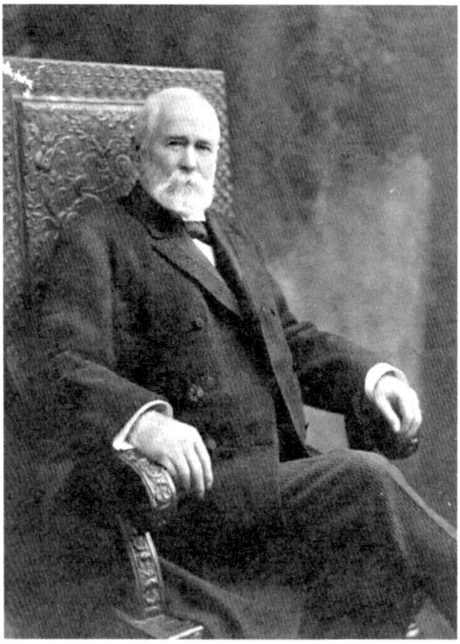

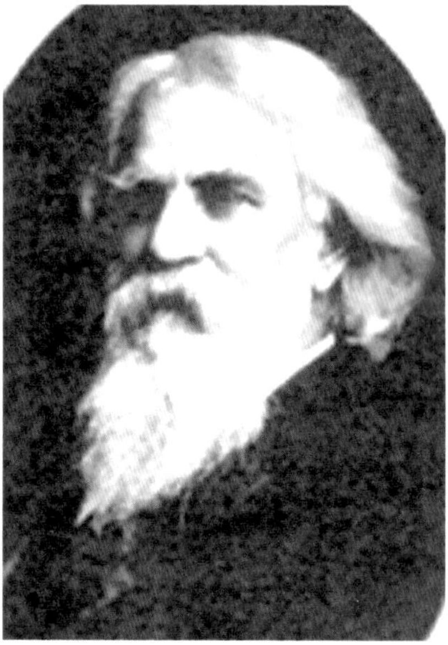

Above left: World-famous billionaire John B. Stetson. Portrait taken sometime before 1906. *Courtesy of the State of Florida Archives—Florida Memory Project.*

Above right: Henry DeLand, the man with a vision of grandeur for Florida to become the "Athens of the United States." *Courtesy of the State of Florida Archives—Florida Memory Project.*

out Henry DeLand, it also stopped him from supporting the town's small college, which at that time was called the DeLand Academy. Stetson picked up where Henry DeLand left off and began supporting the college, by then called Stetson Baptist University (modern-day Stetson University and internationally known as one of the best small institutes of higher learning in the United States).

When the university first opened its doors as a private academy, the board of regents was made up of local Baptist ministers. John Stetson had no problem with this as he was raised a Baptist. Many ministers, missionaries and affluent people from all over the United States applied to send their budding young adult children to Stetson Baptist University—either as a place of higher learning to earn a degree or as a finishing school for some (mostly young woman).

One such family were the Browns, from Iowa. Mr. Brown was a Baptist minister with big plans for his little girl. His daughter Susanna was to attend the new private Baptist University as a finishing school, and hopefully find a worthy beau to marry in the process. When Susanna first

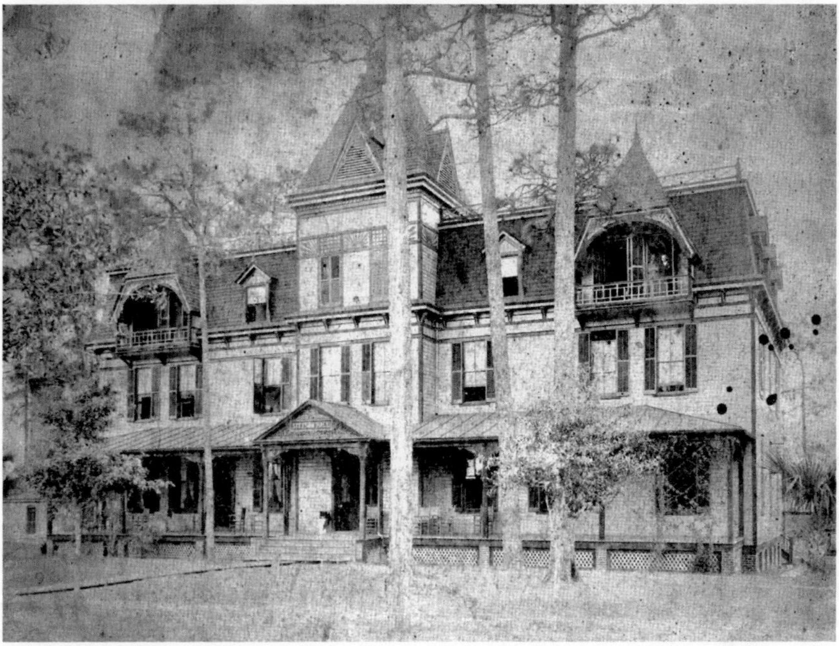

Stetson Hall at Stetson Baptist University, circa 1892. *Courtesy of the State of Florida Archives—Florida Memory Project.*

arrived in the Sunshine State, she had a great deal of trouble adjusting to her new and lonely life. Being raised with nine siblings in a small farming community in the Midwest, she was now faced with a strange new daily life. She tried to make new friends, but was not up on all the current fashions or worldly news like many of the other young women on campus. She quickly fell into a depression and began keeping to her studies and herself.

Susanna's English literature professor noticed the young woman early on in her first semester, and saw how she was always walking, eating and studying alone. One day, while Susanna was walking alone, he decided to begin a conversation with her after class and they both discovered that they were from the same area in Iowa. Instantly, Susanna's whole demeanor began to change. She glowed like the morning sun. She had finally found a new friend on campus. As time passed, the professor and Susanna discussed at length poetry, world events, the mysteries of the universe and life itself. Susanna began to blossom intellectually, emotionally and physically.

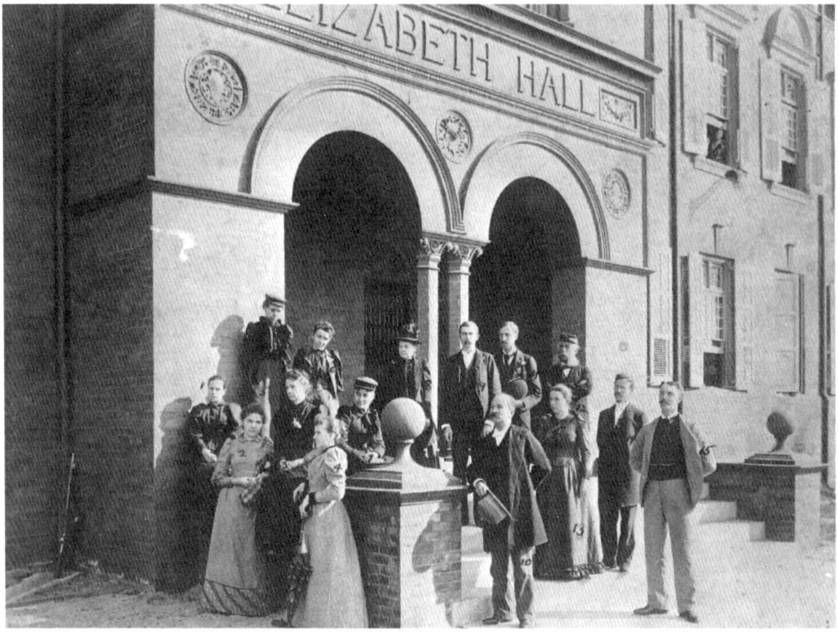

The faculty of Stetson Baptist University at the time Susanna attended school there, circa 1892. The professor is said to be the second man from the right. *Courtesy of the State of Florida Archives—Florida Memory Project.*

One afternoon, while the two walked and talked, the professor leaned down and picked a morning glory flower and handed it to Susanna. Susanna, being young, innocent and ignorant of the fine line between friendship and love, saw this as more than just a friendly gesture—she took it to heart, literally. When she returned to her modest dorm room, she held the flower close to her heart and wished to marry a man just like her dear professor. She then carefully placed the flower in her favorite poetry book and pressed it closed.

As the months passed, time seemed to fly by for Susanna. She now looked forward to attending her classes and even more so to the upcoming summer break. Since her father was a minister supporting several children still at home, Susanna knew she would spend her summer on campus with her professor. She knew that her professor would be teaching several summer classes but that his schedule wouldn't be as demanding as during the other semesters; she knew they would be able to spend more time together.

As Susanna had made it known to the professor when her birthday was, he was kind enough to purchase a hair ribbon for the blossoming young

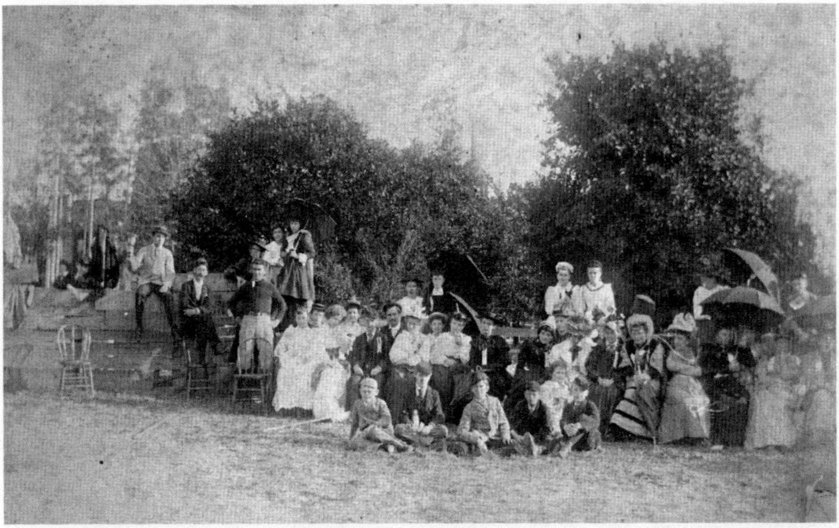

Susanna's life became more social since meeting the professor. She even posed for this photo with other students, circa 1892. Susanna is the second from the right, in the back row. *Courtesy of the State of Florida Archives—Florida Memory Project.*

woman. Susanna treasured this ribbon and wore it nearly every day. She adorned her dark brown hair with the pale green ribbon, wearing it as if it were an engagement ring instead of a mere hair ribbon. Any time she would receive a compliment about how nice the ribbon looked, she would simply nod her head and smile, knowing deep inside that her professor had given her this gift she now treasured.

When the summer sessions began, Susanna took on a part-time job in the library on campus to help pay for her room and board. But there was still plenty of time during her days to have lengthy discussions with her professor between his classes. One afternoon they decided to go down by the lake and have a small picnic lunch while discussing some new works by their favorite authors. During their discussion, her professor handed Susanna an envelope. She held her breath and closed her eyes as she carefully opened the seal on the fine linen envelope. Inside was a beautiful poem simply titled "Susanna." As she read the poem to herself, a tear rolled down her cheek and she realized that her professor had fallen in love with her. Her head told her it was wrong for either of them to feel this way about the other. Not only was he one of her instructors, but he was nearly twenty years her senior. However, her heart didn't care—she knew she loved him and now she knew he loved her. What more should

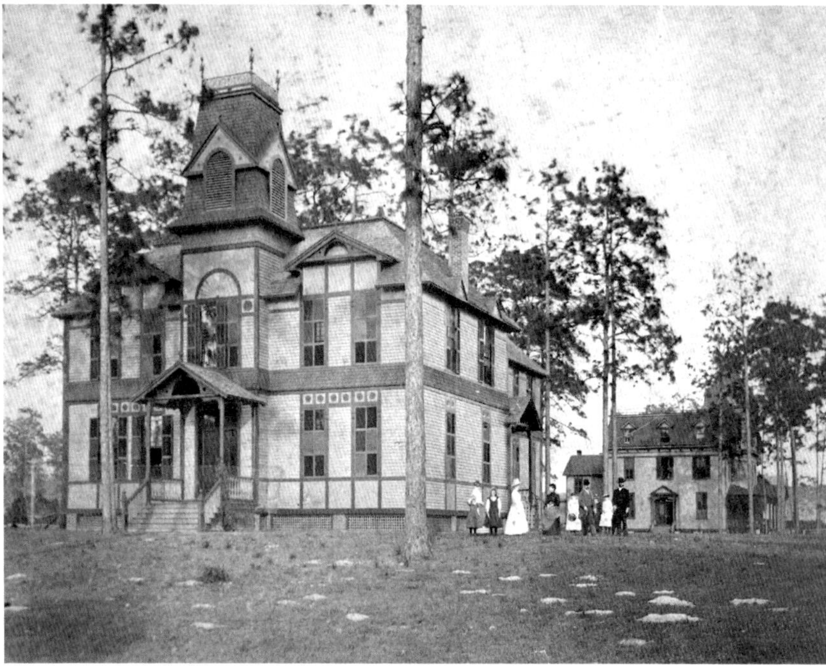

DeLand Hall at Stetson Baptist University, circa 1890. *Courtesy of the State of Florida Archives—Florida Memory Project.*

ever matter? She finished reading the poem, gently held his hand, looked deeply into his eyes and said, "I feel the same way about you."

The couple continued their affair in secret throughout the summer months. By the time the fall session had begun, they were deeply in love. They both realized that they would have to keep their feelings secret. After all, if anyone had ever found out it would mean not only the end of their relationship, but Susanna would most likely be thrown out of school and the professor could be fired from his job—or worse. They agreed to meet every night at the back of Hulley Tower at the stroke of midnight to steal a few moments away together. They chose midnight so that they "could begin each day with one another," as her professor so eloquently worded it.

This plan worked quite well for a short while, until the night when some of the staff that had been to a late-night performance at the nearby Athens Theater returned later than expected. When they witnessed the two lovers embraced in a kiss, they knew the incident would have to be reported to the administration. The professor stood with his head held

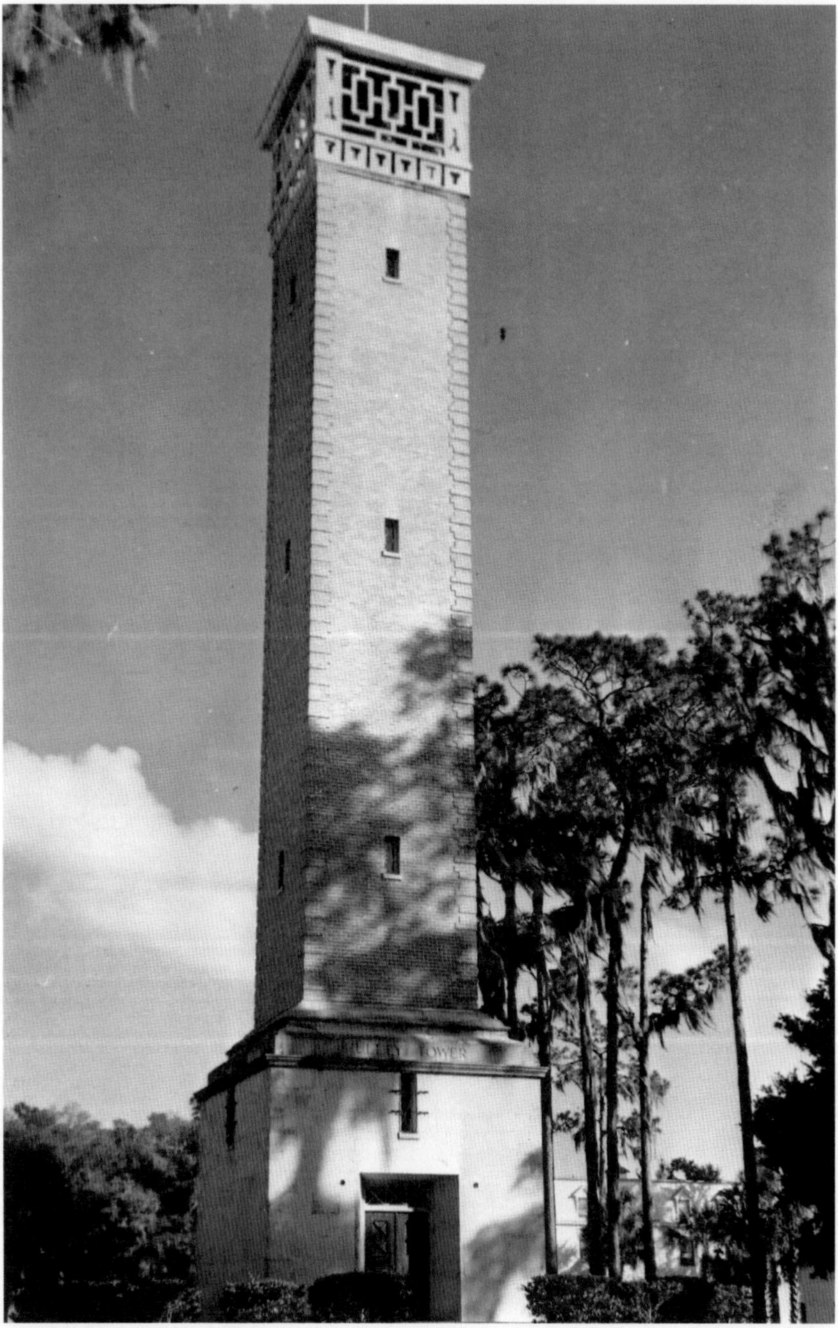

Hulley Tower was the couple's secret nightly meeting place. *Courtesy of the State of Florida Archives—Florida Memory Project.*

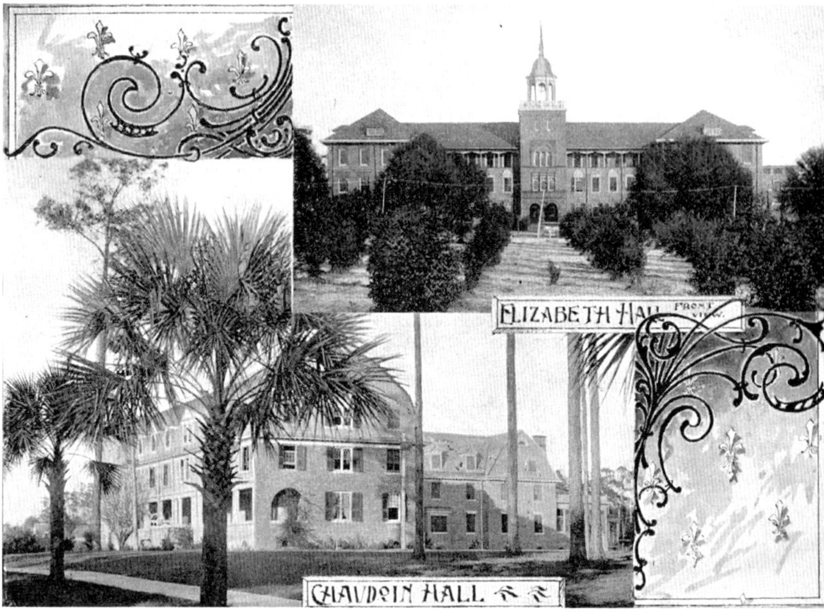

Elizabeth Hall and Chaudion Hall on the campus of Stetson Baptist University, circa 1892. *Courtesy of the State of Florida Archives—Florida Memory Project.*

high—he felt no shame for the feelings he had for his Susanna. Susanna, being young, was not as strong as her professor; she wept incessantly as her dorm mother was called to escort her back to her dorm room.

The following morning, Susanna was brought to the administrator's office, where she was informed that she would need to leave Stetson Baptist University permanently. When she inquired as to the fate of her lover, she was told that he would be quietly leaving his teaching position and would now be doing the Lord's work as a missionary overseas. Susanna then politely inquired if she could speak with her professor before she was made to pack her belongings—her plea was met with only silence and a glaring stare from the administrator.

Susanna was then led across campus to her dorm room in shame, at the busiest time of day on campus, and made to pack her belongings. Her guard left momentarily to inquire of the dorm mother if her father had been informed yet that Susanna would be returning home in "shame and as a disgrace to the family." Susanna sat quietly on her bed for a moment, closed her eyes and formed a picture in her mind of the picnic she and the professor had shared. She opened a small, ornately decorated box and pulled out her pale green hair ribbon, the first poem her professor had written her and the morning glory flower that was now pressed flat and dried.

Without anyone noticing, Susanna left her dorm room and walked purposefully across the campus until she stood at the base of Hulley Tower. She paused for a moment and tied the pale green ribbon into her dark brown flowing hair. She opened the door that led to the stairway of the tower, closing and locking the door behind her, and began to climb the stairs. When she reached the top, she stood on the edge and loudly announced her name and declared her love for the professor. She then read aloud the first poem he had written to her and again professed her love for him. She held the dried flower to her heart, closed her eyes and stepped off the edge of Hulley Tower, falling to her death.

If you visit the campus of Stetson University in the early fall, you may be able to catch a glimpse of the spirit of Susanna Brown. They say that every fall she again climbs the tower and steps off the edge, like she did all those years ago, taking a stand and making a statement of true love to her professor.

Yet another active spirit associated with the small university is that of a man who walks his ghostly dog. Every evening, just as the sun goes down, the figure of an elderly gentleman can be seen walking the misty form a

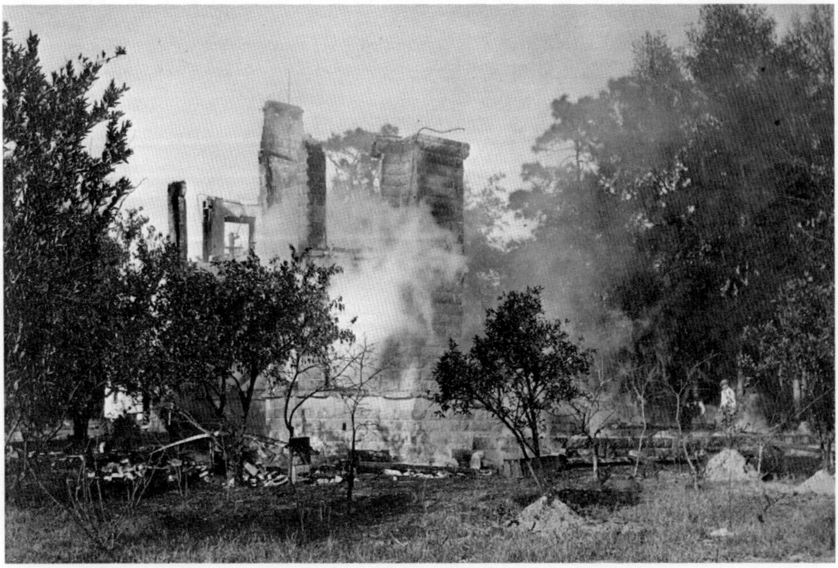

The aftermath of the fire that consumed Conrad Hall and possibly killed the groundskeeper and his dog. *Courtesy of the State of Florida Archives—Florida Memory Project.*

small dog throughout the campus of Stetson University. These two spirits have been joined in the hereafter for many decades, and it is believed that they may be the spirits of a man who was out late one night walking his dog on the campus grounds and was killed by a hit-and-run driver. The dog survived that incident, so no one is quite sure just who the man or the dog are, but they are the most active and most frequently seen spirits on the campus of Stetson University.

Another theory as to the identity of the man and his ghostly companion comes about from a fire that occurred at the university at Conrad Hall. Some of the old-timers in town say that the man worked at the university as a groundskeeper. He lived in a small maintenance shed on the campus grounds with his pet dog. When the fire broke out in Conrad Hall, the groundskeeper was there and raced inside to help other people get out of the building and to do what he could to stop the blaze. His lifelong companion followed him through the front door and both were engulfed in the flames, never to be seen again—or maybe just not seen alive!

Chapter 2

The Ghost of Granny Quigley

Myrtle Quigley was not always a grandmother. When she arrived in the United States from Ireland as a toddler in the mid-1800s at Ellis Island, New York, her family realized that the living situation in New York for immigrants was not the perfect environment in which to raise their young family. They quickly decided to move south to greener pastures and found themselves ending up in central Florida. DeLand was booming at the time with orange groves, honey processing plants, timber and lumber plants, cattle farming, turpentine processing and cotton plantations and turned out to be a great place to raise their family. With the wonderful weather, decent people and fresh air, they quickly settled into a new life and the family soon began to grow.

Myrtle had an older brother when they first arrived in the United States, but by the time she reached the age of twelve, she now had seven younger siblings as well. Since she was the eldest daughter, her mother relied heavily upon her to help with the daily household chores and with raising her younger brothers and sisters. Myrtle didn't mind helping out—she saw these tasks as a form of training for when she would eventually marry and have her own children and she took great pride in every aspect of her chores and put a great deal of energy and love into helping raise her younger siblings.

When Myrtle turned fifteen years old, her life began to drastically change. Her father passed away suddenly and a yellow fever epidemic was running its course through the Southern states. Her family did not fair well. Her older brother had joined the military forces two years before their father passed away and was never seen or heard from again. Her

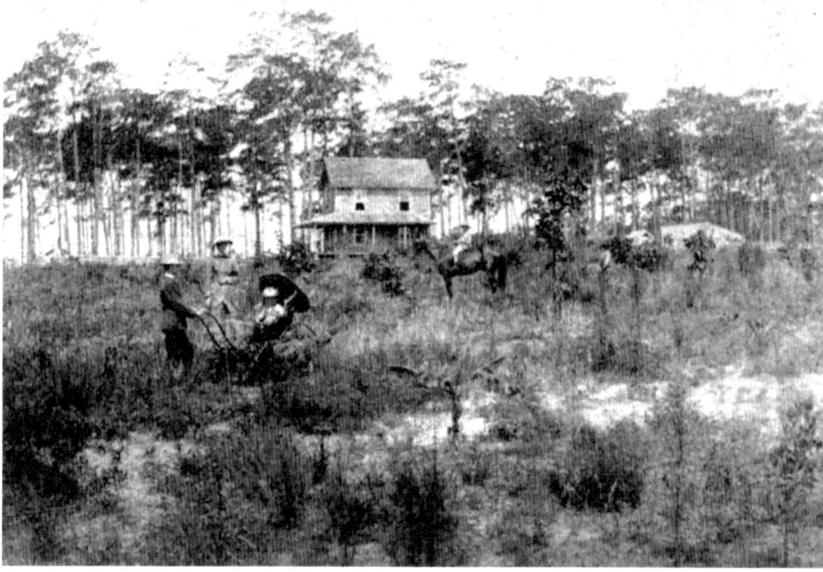

The Quigley family on their new homestead in DeLand. *Courtesy of the State of Florida Archives—Florida Memory Project.*

mother fell into a deep depression and more and more responsibilities began to fall on Myrtle. She now did all the cooking, cleaning and other daily chores by herself, all while taking care of her siblings, now sick from the fever. One by one her brothers and sisters began to succumb to the wretched disease that claimed so many lives.

During this time, on one of her weekly trips to town to purchase supplies, Myrtle met a young man. She didn't notice him at first. She was too focused on completing her shopping chores and returning home to get back to work. She was running through a list in her head of what she needed to attend to when she got home and actually began to recite the list out loud, which is what drew the attention of the young man. He leaned over and politely introduced himself, and when Myrtle looked into his eyes, it was love at first sight. They spoke for a few brief moments and Myrtle finished her order, paid the bill and walked toward the door.

The young man followed her and in his gentlemanly manner opened and held the door for her. He followed her outside and assisted her with strapping the bundles onto her mule. It was at that moment that Myrtle broke down crying. It had been so long since anyone had been kind to her or even spoken to her. The young man quickly wrapped his arms around her, holding her tight and telling her that everything would be all right. He offered to walk her home and she graciously accepted. She had been caring for so many others for such a long time it was nice to finally have someone caring for her, even if it would only last for the short walk home.

When the couple arrived at Myrtle's home, the young man instantly realized that there was no man in the house and that the home badly needed some tender loving care—the kind of care a man of his caliber could help with. He offered to stick around for a while and help out if she would agree to making him a glass of iced tea, the house wine of the South. Myrtle agreed. She went into the house and turned on the kettle, keeping an eye and ear on the goings-on outside. She attended to her family's immediate needs and then brought the glass of iced tea outside. The young man noticed her exiting the front door and stopped working to take a break and drink the cold liquid she had brought him. He wiped the sweat from his brow, sat on the edge of the porch and lifted the glass to his lips. Myrtle said, "I'm so sorry, I was a bit distracted when we met. I don't recall what you said your name is. Would you please tell me again?" Just then he spurted the iced tea out of his mouth all over the porch! Myrtle said, "I'm sorry, did I say something wrong?" The young man began to laugh. "You must really be distracted with your family's troubles. My name is James, you didn't ask anything out of line, and your being distracted caused you to use salt in your iced tea instead of sugar."

Myrtle turned beet red and turned her face away from James. She began to apologize, but he stood up, took her hand and told her it was an honest mistake since the two look very similar and that he understood how she could confuse them, especially with all she had going on in her life. Although she still felt embarrassed, she smiled at him and the love she had begun to feel for him in the store now became very real. From that day forward, James became a permanent fixture at the Quigley home.

Although Myrtle had lost her father, older brother and five of her seven younger siblings, she now had hope back in her life. She and James were married on the steps of the courthouse only three short months after meeting one another. Her mother seemed to get better too. Having

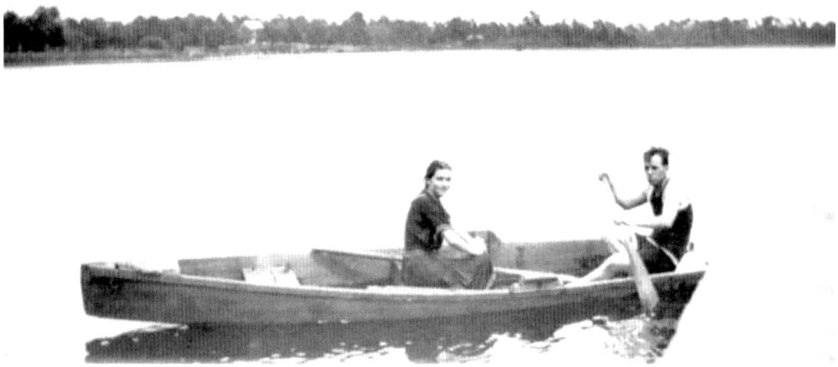

Myrtle and James in a rowboat on the St. John's River after recently marrying. *Courtesy of the State of Florida Archives—Florida Memory Project.*

a man around the house reminded her of her own husband and she was now getting out of bed more often, eating a bit more and even sat in her favorite rocking chair on the front porch from time to time. Life would never be as it was, but now it seemed their lives were headed in a new direction and toward something better.

Myrtle's mother finally passed away of natural causes and her two remaining younger siblings grew up and headed out to begin their own adult lives. Myrtle and James remained in the Quigley family home and began to raise a family of their own. They had two children and, with times being what they were, Myrtle took on a part-time job scrubbing floors and cleaning up at the local bank and at one of the local churches. By the time her children reached their teens, she had cleaning jobs at five local businesses, including two churches. She would get up before dawn, fix the children their bag lunches and head out to work with a handcart full of cleaning supplies. Six days a week she cleaned two bank buildings, one insurance agency building and on Wednesdays and Sundays she would also clean the churches.

As times began to change, Myrtle did too. Her children now grown, she didn't really need the money, but her work kept her busy while James was working, so she continued to work as the local scrubwoman (or so she began to be called). Her work hours changed too. Since her children were now grown and gone, all of her employers asked if she could come in after hours and clean before they opened up the next morning, instead of her old schedule of coming in very early and finishing just as they were coming in. Some of her employers felt with her age, and her slowing down a bit, that this might give her more time to finish her duties without feeling any pressure. Myrtle agreed and began her new routine at work.

James passed away one night when she was still at work. She returned home one morning to find him lying in their bed with their framed wedding photo in his hand. Her heart was broken and she began to change from a politely social woman into somewhat of a recluse. She rarely spoke to people she knew, even when she went to the various local stores to do her shopping. When friends and acquaintances stopped by, she rarely, if ever, answered the door and they eventually gave up and stopped coming by. She kept to herself, her daily routines and her work as the local scrubwoman. It was at this time that folks began calling her "Granny."

Old-timers in the DeLand area still remember Granny. Since she was the local scrubwoman and cleaned the banks, insurance agency and churches, she was quite well known. Granny could be seen seven mornings a week, with her rickety old hand cart, walking home just before sunrise. After so many years of scrubbing floors, she was slightly hunchbacked. She now had a full head of snow-white hair, dark sunken eyes and she dressed appropriately for the jobs she did. She wore long housecoat-style dresses, an apron, a large sun hat and shoes that flopped when she walked, almost as if they were two sizes too large. Some folks mentioned in passing that Granny had taken to wearing James's old shoes after he had passed away to keep him with her at all times. As if Granny wasn't a colorful enough character, she had one more piece of daily attire that made her stand out—she wore an old, tattered, brown leather pouch tied tightly around her waist. The leather bag seemed to always raise an eyebrow or two from onlookers as Granny passed by, most likely because the pouch and its contents were a mystery. People began to notice her pouch well before fanny packs became popular and no one in town had seen anything like this prior to Granny starting a possible new fashion trend. Many people in town assumed she used this leather pouch as a wallet, small purse or more likely as a coin purse.

You could always hear Granny coming as she made her way through the dimly lit streets of DeLand in the early morning hours—pushing her rickety old cart with its wheels squeaking, the cleaning supplies rattling against one another, bottles clinking together and the ever-present sound of jingling coins from the pouch strapped tightly to her waist. With every bump in the sidewalk, you knew Granny was passing by with the almost musical sounds of her cart.

After having such a long, hard life, with only brief moments of hope and happiness, poor hardworking Granny passed away one fine spring morning. She was taken via ambulance to the local funeral parlor and when the undertaker was preparing her for her burial, he noticed her leather pouch was still tied tightly around her waist. Since this was one of her signature fashion statements, he felt it best to leave it with her in her casket. There were few people in attendance at Granny's funeral—a few local shop owners, her longtime employers, a handful of congregation members from the churches she cleaned and the funeral home and cemetery staff, along with a reverend who obviously didn't know Granny well. His sermon and eulogy, while sweet and appropriate, never mentioned who Myrtle Quigley ever really was.

Once the services were over at the funeral parlor, Granny was taken via hearse to Oakdale Cemetery in DeLand to be laid to rest next to her beloved husband James. As Granny's casket was being lowered from the hearse bier to the ground, it slipped and hit the bottom of the freshly dug grave hard with an audible thump! When it did, the few people present could hear the coins jingling from inside the coffin.

As Granny had no family left in the area to speak of, and no one who attended her funeral really knew her—they only attended out of respect for the work she had done for them for many years—the only people in attendance at her burial were the undertaker from the funeral parlor and the local gravedigger. It is said that when the gravedigger turned his back to retrieve his shovel to begin filling in Granny's gravesite, the undertaker quickly reached inside Granny's casket and stole her tattered leather money pouch. After her grave was closed, the gravedigger recalled the undertaker walking away and whistling with a bulge in his pocket, and the sound of jingling coins could be heard as he stepped.

If you visit Oakdale Cemetery on bright, early spring mornings, it is said that if you hold your ear close to Granny's grave, you can still hear her coins jingling from inside her casket, which doesn't make much sense if her leather pouch was truly stolen. It is possible that the gravedigger was wrong and that she did retain her money pouch. We may never know for sure. However, if you happen to be awake in the early hours just before dawn and walk the area near Granny's old route home from work, you can still hear the squeaky wheels, rattling supplies and clanking bottles of Granny's old rickety handcart as her spirit continues to find her way home.

Chapter 3
The Girl in the Lake

Before DeLand became known for its beautiful architecture, private university, cultural arts and affluent people from all over the world, it was an area of pioneer settlers and pioneer justice. Before the old courthouse was first built and the seat of county justice and government were established in DeLand, court and justice were governed by hardened local men, sometimes with very closed minds and hard hearts—the kind of men who had little tolerance for lawbreakers and believed in swift, severe punishments. Some of these men didn't base decisions on the law of the land, but instead held to a code of morals that they felt should be imposed on *all* the local residents. These morals sometimes intruded on honest folks that were just trying to live, work and prosper in the booming DeLand area.

Many lawbreakers and supposedly morally unsound men met an untimely end due to decisions made by these types of early vigilantes. Many sentences involved a short rope, a quick drop and a very tall oak tree. It is said that one such tree still grows at the south end of what is now known as Earl Brown Park. Several lives were reportedly ended from that tree—some with no sound or just reason, some with no reason at all.

During this time of unfair and unchecked pioneer justice, a young man made his way into the area and began tending to his small, newly purchased orange grove on the outskirts of the west side of town. His name was William, but everyone called him Bill. He kept to himself most of the time, but when he ventured into town for supplies he would be sure to be polite to all the townsfolk he met, always tipping his hat to the ladies and nodding his head to the men. He would purchase his needed

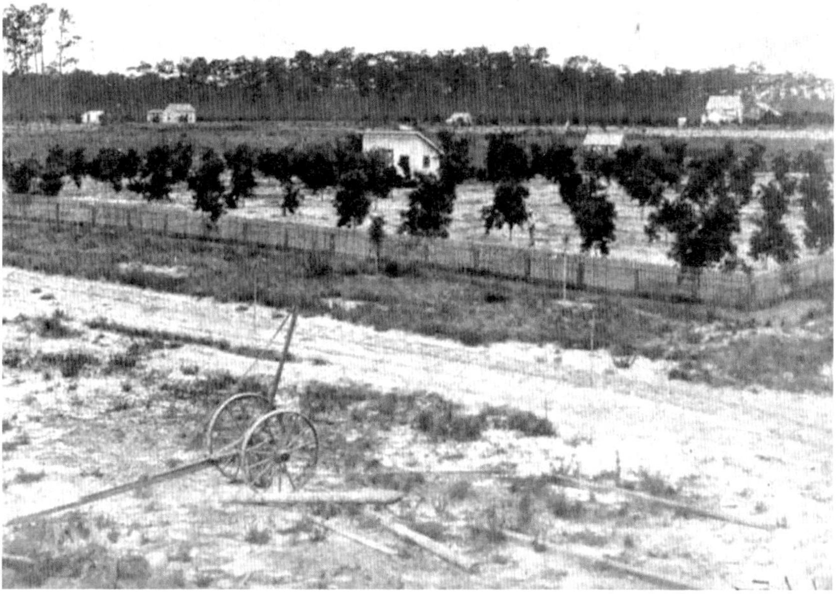

Bill's modest farm and citrus grove on the outskirts of DeLand. *Courtesy of the State of Florida Archives—Florida Memory Project.*

goods, pack them onto his mule and buckboard and head back to his orange grove.

After his groves started to produce, he even became involved in a few trade deals with local merchants for his oranges. Life was good for Bill and he now looked to the future and he hoped to someday meet a nice woman, marry and start a family. He worked hard, attended weekly church services and had a more-than-modest income now. He felt the only thing that could make his life more enjoyable would be the wife and family he had begun to dream about. Now he didn't just go to town and start asking single ladies to marry him; that wouldn't be proper. He quietly paid attention, especially during church socials, as to which young ladies were available. After all, Bill was a good Christian man with good Christian values, and he was looking for the same qualities in his future bride.

During one such social, the church members decided that a picnic near what is now known as Hontoon Island State Park would be a great way to cool off during the summer heat. Bill packed up some sweet, ripe oranges, a pie he attempted to bake and rode his mule over to the swimming and picnic area. He had a wonderful time visiting with other church members, catching up on local news and he even learned a new trick or two about

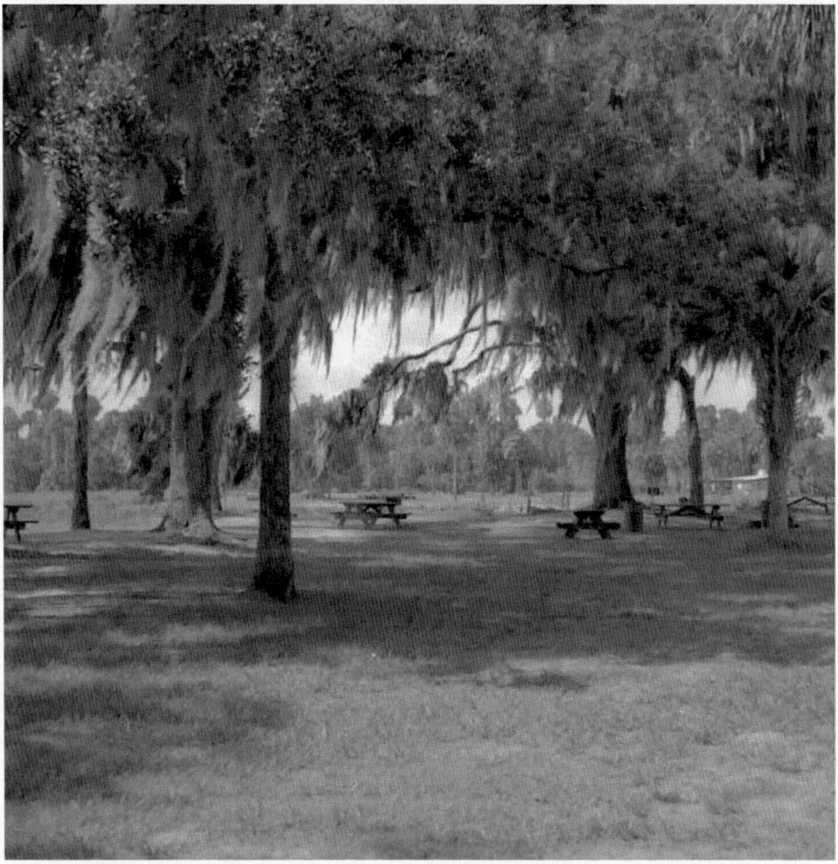

Hontoon Island State Park picnic area as it looked in the 1970s. *Courtesy of the State of Florida Archives—Florida Memory Project.*

keeping insects out of his orange grove. He enjoyed swimming in the cool water, eating his fill of well-cooked food and meeting several people from other churches in the other communities that surrounded DeLand.

While lying on the cool grass, soaking in some sun, he noticed a shadow had come over his closed eyelids. He slowly opened his eyes, and as they adjusted to see the form in his view, he saw the most beautiful young woman he had ever seen. He stumbled a bit getting up and fumbled as he brushed the grass off of his hind end. He finally reached out his hand to the young woman and introduced himself. The young woman bowed her head respectfully and introduced herself as Eliza. She then began to ask Bill if he had baked the pie at the end of the table. Bill raised his eyebrows, smiled and said, "Yes, I baked it myself. Why? Would you care to have the recipe?" Eliza burst out laughing! "No," she said, "I like my pies to be a bit sweeter than yours turned out. You do know that pies are supposed to be on the sweet side?" Bill blushed with embarrassment as he realized that he mistakenly forgot to put sugar into his recipe and that the pie tasted very bland. She forgave him his mistake and confessed to similar mistakes in her early baking days.

The two talked and walked the rest of the afternoon away and when it was time to pack up and head home, Bill offered Eliza a ride home on his mule. She graciously accepted as Bill assisted her with properly getting onto the animal. The couple talked all the way back to town. They discussed some trivial and some not-so-trivial matters of the day and both seemed to be getting to know one another quickly. They shared their dreams and goals, and both realized that they had a great deal in common.

As the couple came to the center of town, the mule trudged past the Wilcox Saloon. They were suddenly taunted by several of the patrons of the saloon. Their conversation came to a halt, but Bill kicked his mule into high gear. About one hundred yards past the saloon, they could still hear the men teasing and taunting the young couple. You see, Bill was the son of a freed African American slave and Eliza was the daughter of a white banker in town. This simply wasn't done or socially acceptable at that time.

Bill stopped his mule at the end of the dirt path leading up to her home. She thanked him for the conversation, and he thanked her for the cooking tips. The two agreed to meet again the following Sunday afternoon, after church of course, and get to know one another even better. Eliza gave Bill a quick kiss on the cheek, jumped down off the mule and ran all the

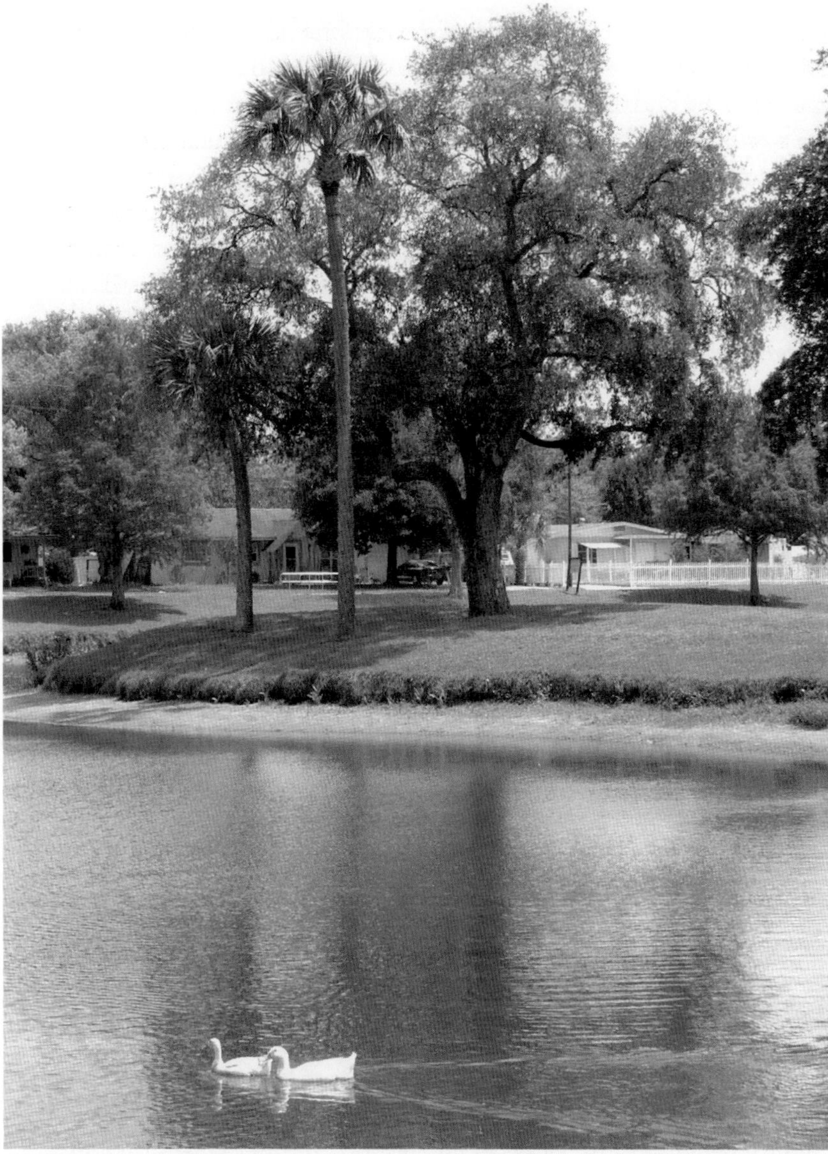

The infamous "hanging tree" in Earl Brown Park as it looks today. *Courtesy of the author.*

way up to the front porch of her home. Bill blushed as he turned his mule around and headed to his own home.

That night, as Bill lay in his bed with thoughts of Eliza racing through his head, he heard a terrible noise out near the barn. He jumped from the bed, grabbed his shotgun and raced out the backdoor of his home, heading for the barn. As he bolted through the barn door he was faced with the same men from the saloon that had taunted him earlier that day. One had a club, one a burlap sack and another held a rope. Before Bill could say a word, get a shot off or make a move of any sort, they began to beat poor Bill until he could barely move. They placed the burlap sack over his head, laid him across the back of his mule and led the mule out of the barn.

The following morning, Eliza woke with high hopes and a smile a mile wide. She decided to go into town to purchase some fabric to make a new dress for the next time she would see Bill. She bought a lovely white fabric with small yellow flowers on it, and began to walk home. As she turned the corner, she noticed a group of people standing and pointing toward the end of the lake. When she made her way to the front of the crowd, she looked up and saw Bill hanging by his neck in the old oak tree.

Heartbroken, she dropped the fabric and ran all the way home. She locked herself in her room and refused to eat or speak to anyone. The following Sunday, the day she was supposed to meet Bill, she attended church, crying and praying for a way to understand the tragedy the entire time. When the services ended, she left alone, walking toward the lake. Her parents and minister thought it best to let her be, but followed close behind to keep an eye on her. They didn't want the men from the saloon to target Eliza next. When they came around the south end of the lake, they saw what appeared to be Eliza standing on the opposite shore. She was dripping wet and looked to be covering herself in mud. The closer they got, the faster Eliza applied the dark earth to every inch of her body. When they got close enough to see that it truly was Eliza, she began to walk out into the lake.

By the time her father jumped into the lake, Eliza was all ready in water up to her shoulders, and she continued to walk out farther. The water finally and completely covered Eliza and all anyone could see was murky water that had mixed with the mud that once entirely covered Eliza. Her father finally found her body but it was too late—Eliza had drowned.

If you go to the lake at Earl Brown Park in the late summer and stand on the south side of the lake, you may catch a glimpse of Eliza's spirit entering the waters of the lake once more. If you look closely, you can still see the murky, muddy water at the lake's center, bubbling and churning with what appears to be blonde hair—this is the exact spot where Eliza took her own life.

Chapter 4
Spirits on the Courthouse Steps

Volusia County is one of Florida's largest counties. The name "Volusia" comes from Volusia Landing on the St. Johns River, where a treaty was signed with the Native American Seminole tribe. Beyond that, the origins of the name are somewhat unclear, though many sources believe it originates from an early settler and a French tradesman named "Veluche." African Americans recently freed from slavery and Northerners began to settle in the area, and by 1869 a town called Spring Hill had developed into what is now DeLand.

Like any city, over the years, DeLand has faced many triumphs and many tragedies. When Volusia County was carved from the larger areas of Mosquito, Orange and Enterprise Counties, Henry DeLand donated the land on which the new courthouse and county seat would be built. After literally wrestling the county seat away from Enterprise, DeLand became the seat of Volusia County in 1888. The architecture of the Volusia County courthouse building tells of the prosperity and opulence of the time period and of Henry DeLand, the man who dreamed that DeLand would be the Athens of Florida (and moreso the entire United States). Little did he know how his dream would turn into a nightmare for one couple less than a century later.

In the early 1980s, a local couple had petitioned the court for a dissolution of marriage. It seems that the husband was a jealous man with a violent temper, and after only a few short years of being married, the wife now feared for her life. Their lives weren't always so tumultuous and, like many young couples in love, the newly married young woman overlooked some very serious warning signs that could have prevented her from ever marrying this man in the first place.

As early as their second date, she had been accused by him of flirting with another man in the restaurant. She began to argue her case, but of course got no where, and decided it was best to drop the subject and just forget that it ever happened. After all, he had worked a lot of overtime that week to be able to afford to take her to this nice dinner—who was she to argue with him? She didn't even have a job. If it weren't for him, she'd be sitting at home eating a frozen dinner right then.

As the relationship progressed, the accusations became more frequent, his anger worsened and he slowly and methodically began cutting her off from friends and family. After only six short months of marriage, she was now alone except for him. He became her entire world, but no matter how hard she tried, it was never good enough. No matter what she cooked, it was never as good as his mother used to make. No matter how clean she kept their home, it was never quite clean enough. Nothing she did ever measured up to his expectations and his verbal, emotional and psychological abuse seemed to increase at a breakneck pace. Just when she thought it couldn't get any worse, the beatings began.

After one year of marriage and now into the early stages of her second pregnancy, she started to fear for the lives of her children and how his actions would affect them. He hadn't hit the children yet. She got back in touch with an old high school friend who talked to her every afternoon and tried his best to counsel her. It helped her to know that someone in the world did care about what she was going through, but she still couldn't bring herself to just leave. She had no money of her own, her name wasn't even on their bank account and she had no car and nowhere to go. How could she leave with an infant, another on the way and no resources?

Finally, when the bruises became too obvious to even cover up with any amount of makeup, she made the decision to leave. She packed a few small items, grabbed all the money from the spare change jar, put the baby in the stroller and headed out the door for the police station. She filled out the sign-in sheet and waited for her name to be called. After what seemed like hours, an officer motioned for her to come to the window. She walked up with her baby in her arms and began to cry, explaining what had been going on. The officer could see the bruises on her face and asked a female officer to take over. She was taken to a woman's shelter, given a small room at a safe house and received medical care, prenatal care and counseling. She knew then it was time to end the marriage and was assisted with filing for a divorce from her husband, who was, of course, livid with the news.

During the court proceedings, the judge warned him several times about his angry outbursts, attitude and threats made against his wife. The wife finally had to have a restraining order placed on her husband, as she feared that he might take her life, given his increasingly violent threats. The paper restraint meant nothing to the man and he continued to harass his wife. He followed her home after court one day to find the address where she now resided. He would call her at all hours of the night and early morning, stop by unannounced, leave dead flowers on her doorstep and even mailed her a package containing a dead fish. The wife finally had enough of his sick games and the authorities arrested him and he was sent to jail for thirty days. This was supposed to stop him from harassing her but it had the opposite effect.

While still incarcerated at the county jail, he received a letter containing his final court date to finalize the dissolution of marriage. Two days after he was to be released from jail, he would be expected to attend the final court date for the divorce. The judge apparently had made all of the necessary decisions in the matter and would be informing the couple as to what those decisions were on that date.

The wife sat nervously next to her attorney, wringing her hands and trying not to make any eye contact with her soon-to-be ex-husband. The husband sat expressionless on the other side of the courtroom; he almost looked as if he wasn't even breathing. The bailiff finally called the court to order and the judge entered the courtroom and took his place behind the bench. As he went through their divorce petition point by point, he explained why he had made the decisions he made. The wife seemed to become a bit more relaxed and she now held her attorney's forearm and squeezed it briefly with every decision that was made in her favor. Since the judge's decisions were, for the most part, made in favor of the wife to protect her and their children, she finally began feeling that she would be safe from this excessively abusive man.

The husband still sat with no expression on his face. He just continued to stare blankly at the judge. When the judge was finished speaking, he asked if both parties understood the decisions he had just stated. The wife said, "Yes," but the husband just stared at the judge. The judge asked the man again if he understood the decisions made by the court, but still received no response from the man. The judge, now tired of this man's games, smacked his gavel down on the bench and asked the man a third

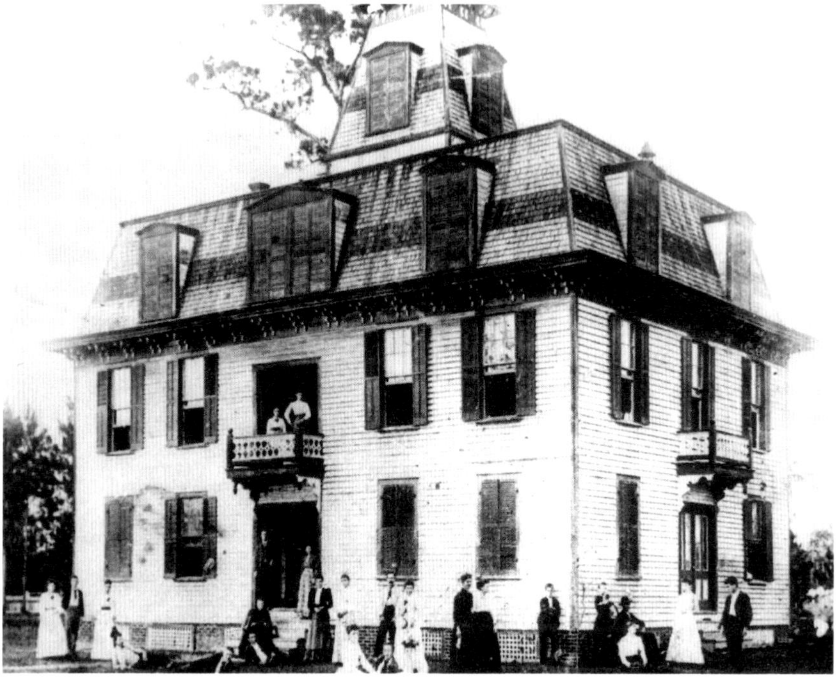

The first Volusia County Courthouse, built in 1887 on land donated by Henry DeLand after Volusia won the county seat over Enterprise. *Courtesy of the State of Florida Archives—Florida Memory Project.*

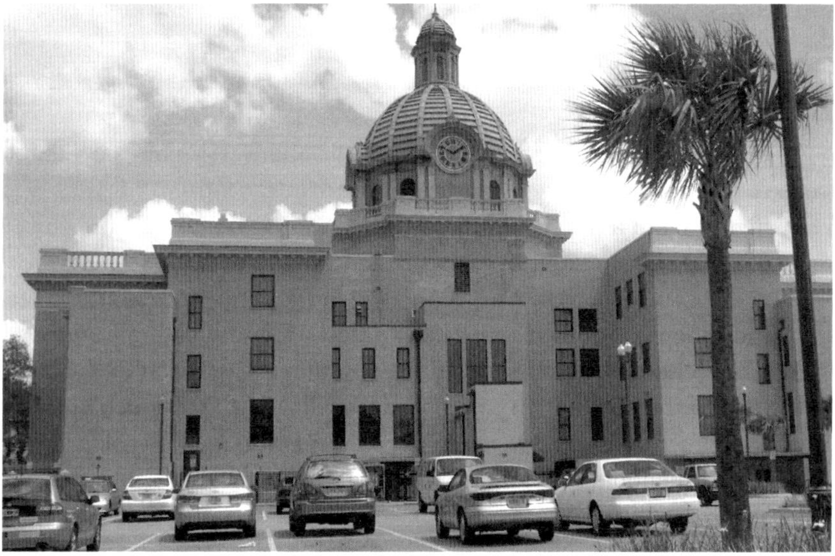

The new Volusia County Courthouse as it still looks in 2008. *Courtesy of the author.*

time. The husband finally nodded in agreement. The judge accepted the nod as acknowledgement of his decisions and finalized the case that ended the marriage and the way of life this man knew.

The woman thanked the judge on the way out of the courtroom and turned to hug her attorney. Her attorney motioned to one of the bailiffs and the bailiff walked over. The attorney instructed the officer to keep the husband in the courtroom until he could safely escort the woman to his car. The bailiff told the attorney that he couldn't promise anything, but said that he would do his best to detain the man.

Several minutes later, as the woman and her attorney were walking down the courthouse steps, almost reaching the bottom step, the ex-husband suddenly burst through the courthouse doors. As he did, he reached into the waistband of his pants and pulled out a pistol. He stared at his wife with pure hatred and held the gun steadily aimed at her. He immediately began shooting at his ex-wife and her attorney. The attorney was hit first—he caught a bullet in the shoulder and fell onto the steps. The woman tried to hide behind her attorney as he fell, but only managed to get him shot again, this time in the chest.

As she slowly stepped away from the severely injured attorney, her ex-husband began to speak. He said, "If I can't have you, no one will!" And he fired one shot directly at his wife's heart. The bullet struck her in the chest and she fell backward down the few remaining courthouse steps. As she lay there dying on the sidewalk, her ex-husband walked over to her and gently held her hand. He stroked her hair and placed her wedding band back on the ring finger of her left hand. He leaned over and kissed her cheek and said, "Remember when we both said 'till death do us part'? This is where we part." He raised the pistol to his own temple and shot himself in the head. His body slumped across his dead wife and the two appeared to be in a sort of twisted, bloodied embrace.

There have been numerous reports of people claiming to find a simple gold wedding band at the bottom of the steps of the courthouse but, when they go to take it out of their pocket, purse or wallet to show it someone else or turn it in, it is no longer there. It is also said that if you come to the courthouse in the early spring months, before the rainy season begins, you can still see the faded chalk outline of the two bodies lying just at the foot of the courthouse steps.

Chapter 5

Do Spirits Still Perform at the Athens Theater?

L.M. Patterson moved to DeLand in 1920 from his native home of Washington, D.C. He purchased land and made preparations to build his dream theater. Patterson initially organized the DeLand Moving Picture Company and had visions of grandeur for opening a magnificent theater in the area. Patterson commissioned an Orlando architect named Murray King to design the Athens Theater in 1921. The facility first opened its doors on January 6, 1922, and the show included a live theater performance, a film and several vaudeville acts. Patterson decided that the theater's name would be derived from the vision of Henry DeLand, the founder of DeLand, who sought to create a city that would be the Athens of the United States—Patterson's theater indeed rivaled the opulence of many upscale theaters worldwide.

Originally opening as a vaudeville house, the Athens Theater featured live stage shows by touring performers, as well as showing black-and-white silent films of the day, eventually showing full color "talkies" with live performers on stage—this may well be the origins of the kind of phenomenon that some of us remember in *The Rocky Horror Picture Show*, which became a pop-culture icon in the late 1970s. Accompaniment from the theater's Wurlitzer pipe organ also thrilled theatergoers.

During the depression, the Athens Theater was the only entertainment people were able to afford. The DeLand Amusement Corporation charged only nine cents for children because if the price were raised to a dime, the corporation would be forced to pay the state entertainment tax. In later years, promotions with the RC Cola Company allowed patrons to enter the theater for free with six RC Cola bottle caps. By this time, the Athens

Theater had become the entertainment centerpiece of the city. The theater continued to operate continuously for nearly seventy years, evolving into a movie house and later a dinner theater. After a renovation in the 1950s, the building deteriorated and eventually closed in the early 1990s.

During the peak of the Athens Theater's heyday and the infancy of B–horror movies, the Athens Theater began to cater to a spookier clientele and offered an interesting and unique new genre of movies combined with live shows. The theater's management also came up with creative new ways of attracting ticket buyers. One such way was to have the audience watch a horror movie while live stage performers would interact with the audience during the film; after all was said and done, the theater guests could spend the night for a pajama party.

At this time, a gentleman by the name of Harry W. Wise—or, as he was better known throughout the world, "Wise the Wizard"—did his midnight ghost show called "Dr. Jekyll & his Weird Show." Wise the Wizard is world famous for this performance and at one time was the only professional stage magician performing a true ghost show in the United States. Another show he performed at the Athens Theater was called "Monsters Crash the Pajama Party," and this required a live performance during the showing of a movie.

In 1964, Wise the Wizard and his troupe of performers played the Florida State Theater Chain, which included doing his midnight ghost show at the Athens Theater in DeLand, the Florida and the Boulevard Theaters in Daytona Beach, the Ritz in Sanford, the Pix in Palatka, the Beach and the Imperial Theaters in Jacksonville and many others.

When Mr. Wise arrived at the Athens Theater in November of 1966 to do the pajama party, he found himself facing a small problem. The movie that was to be shown had a large gorilla in it, and during the show, the gorilla would have to appear to come out of the movie screen, grab a young woman from the audience and take her back into the movie screen. However, he had no young woman that his suited-up gorilla could grab. After all, the gorilla couldn't grab someone who wasn't in on the routine. They might get upset, hit the man inside the suit, have a coronary or worse.

Mr. Wise went to the front office to seek assistance from the management when he saw a young woman at the concession stand. After explaining the "gag" to her, young Margaret Gee agreed to assist with the show—she was only fifteen at the time. The gentleman that played the gorilla was none other than renowned escape artist John Valentine, who was Mr. Wise's partner at the time. Another renowned act that played

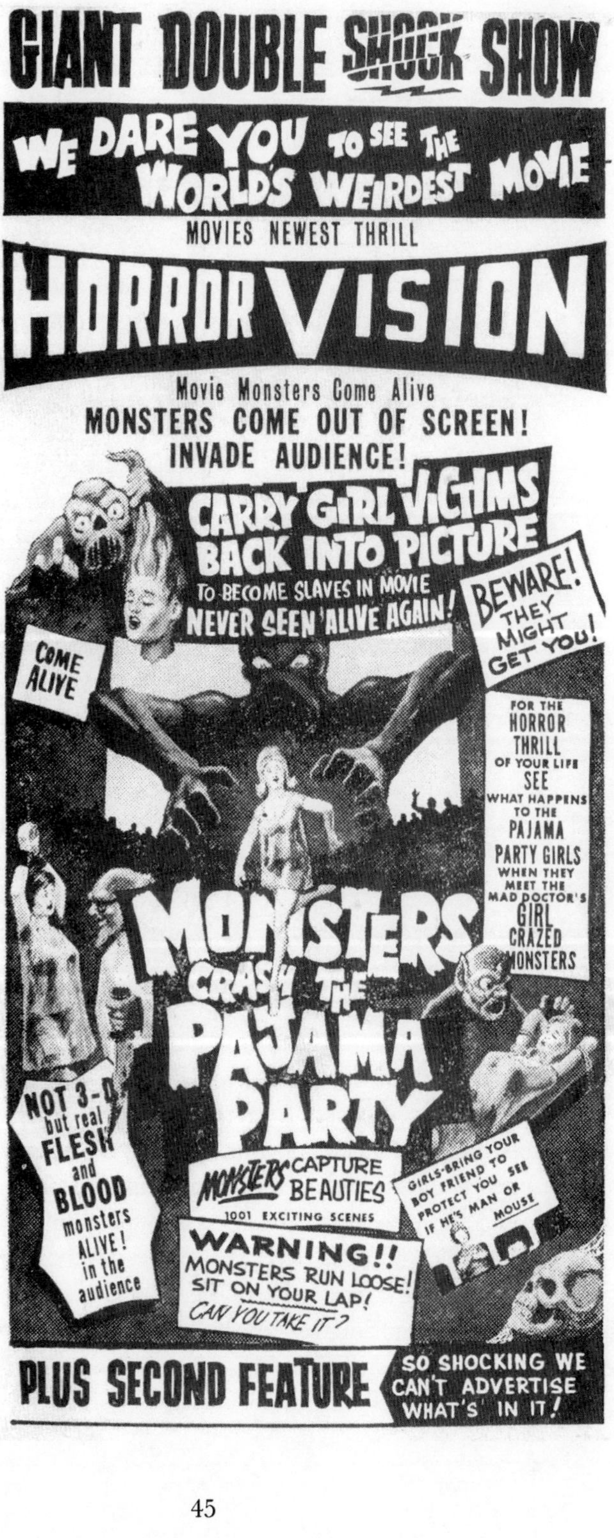

Playbill from "Dr. Jekyll & his Weird Show," held live at the Athens Theater in 1964. *Courtesy of Harry W. Wise.*

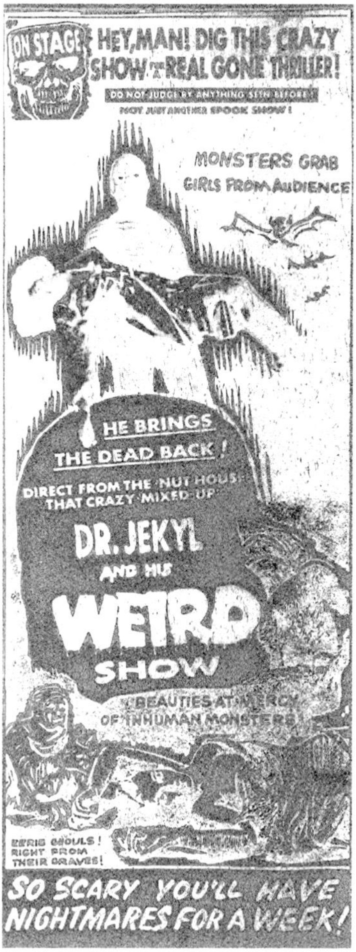

Original playbill from the "Monsters Crash the Pajama Party" live show with "Wise the Wizard" in 1966. *Courtesy of Harry W. Wise.*

the Athens Theater was none other than Dr. Neff and his Madhouse of Mystery. Bill Neff just so happened to be the brother-in-law of world-famous actor Jimmy Stewart, who at one time did movie theater trailer advertising for Bill. The show and live act went off without a hitch and everyone in the audience believed that a gorilla had really taken young Margaret out of the audience and hidden her away.

Margaret, who married Mr. Wise's best friend, still lives in DeLand, while John Valentine now resides in Miami, Florida. Wonderful Wise the Wizard still lives in Sanford, Florida, where he is known as "Sanford's walking artifact." He has a memorial tree planted in Toughey Park across from his home and enjoys the quieter times of being recently retired after a long and varied career as a stage magician, circus performer and one of the only true ghost show operators ever to have worked in the United States.

Over the years, the Athens has served many functions in the community other than being just a fine theater. It was the social center for locals in its early days and in the 1950s—movies, many with the live shows and cartoons, entertained young and old residents alike. There were sack races down the aisles and talent shows on the stage and many locals still fondly remember those bygone days. Some even remember it as the site of their first date and even their first kiss!

In 1994, the Main Street DeLand Association purchased the building and began the long and very costly restoration of this historic theater. After three longs years of hard work, the final touch would be to again light the large marquee out front and the Athens Theater would again be dedicated in a grand ceremony in November of 1997.

One theory as to why there is spirit activity at the Athens Theater is because so many locals have fond memories and strong emotional attachments to the theater. Another theory is that because the performers were so attached to their art form, they chose to stay behind and make sure that the show would always go on. What we do know of the spirits of the Athens Theater is that they remain very active.

One of the spirits is believed to be that of a stagehand that once worked here at the Athens Theater. While assisting other workers in the balcony during the restoration in the 1950s, it is said that he fell to his death in the rows of seats below. The odd thing about his death is that his tool belt became caught on the railing and he swung back and forth for several minutes as he held on for his life. The other workers tried desperately to free the man, but the belt finally gave way and he died from injuries sustained in the fall.

To this day, if you stand in the balcony of the Athens Theater, it will begin to sway back and forth, back and forth. It doesn't matter if the balcony has two people or is fully seated—the swaying still occurs. Some believe that it is the spirit of the stagehand still trying to hold on to his life.

Another active spirit here is that of a young woman that was once a leading actress to a long-running show. Her talents both onstage and off were recognized by the stage manager of the theater. It seems that while the two were having a secret love affair, the stage manager's jealous wife discovered just how talented the young actress was. While paying an unannounced visit to the theater one night, the manager's wife opened the dressing room door to find the two lovers with their unmentionables around their ankles. The young actress, half clothed, began screaming violently at the stage manager's wife. The stage manager tried to explain his actions to his wife and tried to calm both women at the same time—this tactic did not work.

The young actress smacked his face and shoved him out of her dressing room; it seems that the stage manager had neglected to mention to her that he actually had a wife. The two women were now engaged in a very heated argument that would soon turn violent and deadly. The stage manager's wife accused the young actress of leading her husband astray, calling her a harlot and a homewrecker. The actress defended the affair, stating that the wife was a "frigid old fish," not wanting to back down and admit that she had no idea her lover was even married. The argument

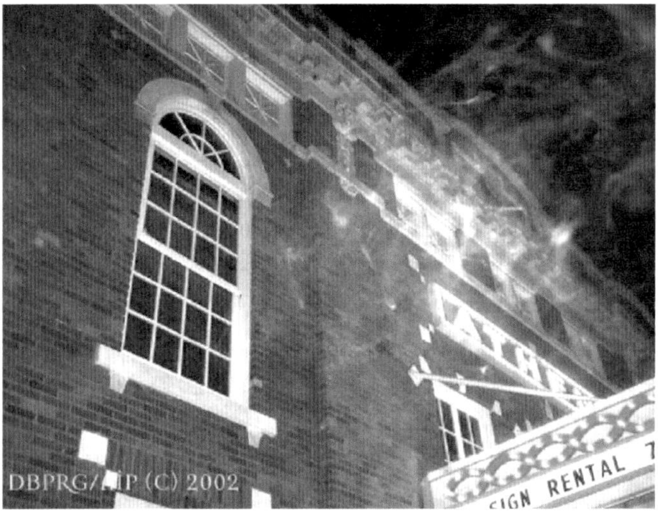

The Athens Theater with an ectoplasmic mist taken during an investigation of the theater in 2002. *Courtesy of the author.*

between the two escalated and finally reached a fevered pitch. With no forethought, the wife grabbed a brass lamp used as a stage prop and bludgeoned the young actress to death.

If you visit the Athens Theater and are lucky enough to get into the dressing room area, beware! This angry spirit does not like the living intruding into *her* dressing room of the afterlife. She has been known to change the room temperature by twenty to thirty degrees Fahrenheit in a matter of seconds, throw large heavy objects at women whom she perceives as a threat and has even been heard singing, laughing and eerily moaning and screaming in several locations throughout the Athens Theater.

Chapter 6

The Spirit of John Fisher—Pharmacist in the Afterlife

The building located at 100 South Woodland Boulevard was at one time the local pharmacy in DeLand. It was a great place to get a root beer float, a quick bite to eat, an ice cream sundae or grab last-minute sundries. You could have your prescriptions filled or find a magazine or book to read, and since it was located in the center of town, it also became a sort of meeting place for many of the local residents. Many locals would visit the store after church on Sunday to grab a bite to eat and catch up on local news and gossip. On Saturdays, dozens of the children would stop in to buy penny candy and families would stop in for a late lunch in the afternoon before heading to the movie theater. The employees knew all their regular customers by name, and all three pharmacists knew what each individual's regular ailments were. It was a living Norman Rockwell painting.

Being centrally located and so popular with the residents of the DeLand area, there were three full-time pharmacists on duty every day of the week. The owner and head pharmacist was a man by the name of John Fisher. John was a highly respected member of the community that took his job as a pharmacist very seriously. He was personable and really cared about the fine folks he aided—he was even known to make deliveries of needed medications at all hours of the day and night on his own time off.

One bright sunny Sunday afternoon in the 1950s, there was a lull in the activity in the store. All three pharmacists, including John Fisher, were on duty. Two of the pharmacists were busy filling prescriptions for their clients who depended on their accuracy and prompt service, while one of

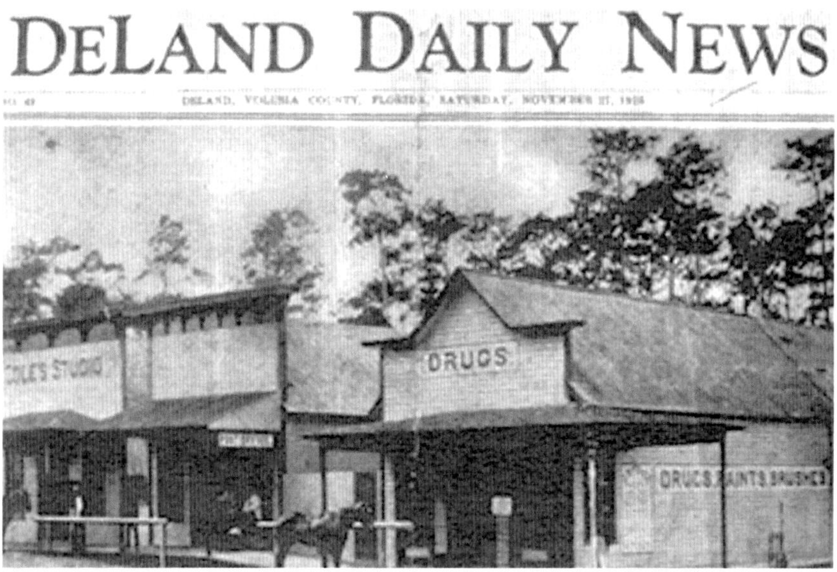

The exterior of Fisher's Drug Store when it was a community meeting place. *Courtesy of Opal Lee.*

them was restocking shelves and taking inventory so an order could be placed the following day.

Earlier that week, John had hired a young handyman to do some upgrading in the backroom of the store. The workman showed up on time and ready to get working on the task ahead of him even though it was Sunday—the job needed to be finished before the new week began. He carried his toolbox and John explained to him what needed to be done and showed the workman to the back storeroom. As the workman began his job, John and the two other pharmacists returned to attending to their own work.

Early in the afternoon, a customer came through the front door and yelled, "Just me John! Gonna look at the new magazines, pay me no mind." John acknowledged him with a wave and said, " Enjoy yourself, just give me a holler if you need anything," and he went back to filling the numerous prescriptions in front of him.

Several minutes later, one of John's assistants commented about hearing a strange hissing noise coming from behind them. John looked at him over the top of his glasses and said, "When is the last time you had your hearing checked? I don't hear anything but the fans." Just then the workman ran through the building and out the rear side door. The

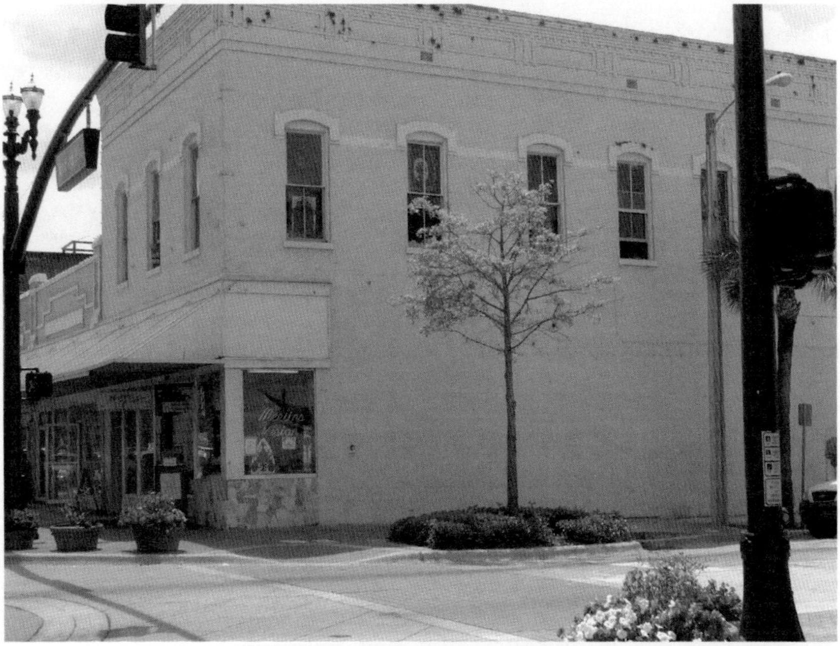

Fisher's Drug Store in 2008 is now Merlin's Vision, a metaphysical shop. *Courtesy of the author.*

assistant pharmacist that was stocking the shelves commented about the fact that he must have needed to use the restroom as he left the odd odor of rotten eggs behind him as he ran by. The three men giggled at the comment.

Suddenly there was a loud explosion and the store was instantly engulfed in flames. The workman was blown away from the rear entrance of the building and people came from all directions to try to help those caught in the blast inside. The fire department was quick to arrive on the scene and realized that a gas line had somehow been cut in the rear of the building. They turned the gas line off and got the fire under control. They would later find out that the workman John Fisher had hired had accidentally cut the line, which not only caused the explosion and fire, but also explained the hissing sound and smell of rotten eggs. The workman had run out to shut the gas off, but did not accomplish his task in time.

Half of the downtown business district went up in flames. The fire destroyed over 60 percent of the town's original layout and buildings. Many businesses were burned completely to the ground and it took many years to rebuild. Much of the town never recuperated from that fire. An older law was soon amended after this devastating fire and was immediately put into effect that *no* buildings in the downtown business district would be allowed to be built from anything other than brick. No wooden buildings would ever be allowed in that area of town again.

As the flames finally diminished, the firefighters discovered four people had been in the drugstore building at the time of the initial blast and ensuing inferno. John Fisher's two assistant pharmacists and the customer reading magazines were rushed to the local hospital but all died from their severe burns and other injuries they received during the tragic fire. John Fisher died at the scene of the fire as he was the closest to the blast.

With John Fisher's death, the pharmacy died as well. It would never again be the living image of a Norman Rockwell painting that it once was. It did reopen as a drugstore for a while, but never regained the momentum or clientele it once had. Eventually the store became Merlin's Vision, a New Age store that offered everything from incense and candles to books on astrology and herbal remedies. John Fisher, however, is still keeping track of customers and business in *his* old drugstore building. Current and some past owners of the building all describe a man that fits John Fisher's description being seen in the area of the store where the prescriptions used to be filled. They describe a man in his late fifties to early sixties, wearing a white druggist's smock–style shirt, black rimmed eyeglasses and dark, thinning hair. He always glances at the employees over the top of his glasses, turns and then disappears.

In the backroom area of the building, where the deadly fire started, it is always a few degrees higher than the temperature in the rest of the store. Strange hot breezes from nowhere blow through the building when no doors have been opened; when current employees mix medicinal herbs together, John Fisher's spirit is ever watchful. If they make an improper decision in the combination of herbs they are mixing together, in John Fisher's opinion, he will quickly knock the jars over or he will even sometimes make the correct jar fall off the shelf. This is just John Fisher's spirit's way of still caring for the customers of the old DeLand drugstore.

Chapter 7

The Energetic Creature in the Masonic Temple Building

The oldest Masonic Temple in the world is in England. It was built during the fifteenth century and still operates fully today. When Europeans began arriving in the New World, many Masons were among them. In Europe, the brotherhood of Masons had so much political power at one time that when the English Parliament made it a law that oath-taking brotherhoods could not exist, the Masons were given an exemption in the law.

Membership in the brotherhood of Masons means many things. It means being part of an unbroken tradition that stretches back over five hundred years to a time when guilds of freemasons traveled throughout Europe, laying the stones of the great Gothic cathedrals. It means sharing the values of our nation's founding fathers—the ideals of men who believed in the brotherhood of man are firmly rooted in the Constitution of the United States. It means becoming a better person while helping to improve the quality of life for others. It means forming deep and lasting friendships that transcend the boundaries of race, religion and culture, as well as those of geography. But most of all, being a Mason signifies the kind of deep satisfaction that comes only from selfless giving, from doing for others without asking or expecting anything in return.

In its early years, Masonry numbered among its members some of the nation's most influential citizens, among them such people as George Washington, Henry Knox, Benjamin Franklin, John Hancock and Paul Revere. Many of the Patriots who participated in the Boston Tea Party were believed to be Masons, and others sacrificed their lives in the struggle for independence from British rule. The values that were important then—values such as loyalty, patriotism, liberty, courage and faith—are just as important to Masons today. The principles upon which this country was founded are deeply embedded in being a member of the Masons.

Freemasonry is built upon three basic tenets: Brotherly Love, Relief and Truth. Brotherly Love is the practice of the golden rule. Relief embodies charity for all mankind. Truth is honesty, fair play and adherence to the cardinal virtues. These moral lessons are taught during three ceremonies, or "degrees," via allegory and symbolism, using the traditional stonemason's tools.

The First Degree uses the gavel and gauge to remind the new member of his dependence on others and his subordination to a higher power. In the Second Degree, the square, level and plumb are used to reinforce the moral lessons of brotherly love and service. Then in the Third Degree, the trowel and other tools encourage the candidate to reflect on the end of life and on the value of faithfulness to his promises.

Freemasonry, while believed by most to be a secret society, is claimed by its members to not be a secret organization of any kind. While lodge buildings are clearly marked and listed in the phone book and members frequently wear rings and pins identifying them as Masons, Masonry members value confidentiality and, as with many other organizations, many of its meetings are not open to the public, including initiation rites and rituals. During these first three degrees of oath-taking and rituals, there are some secrets that the Masons do not share with the general public. These oaths and rituals, some believe, can create an energy that is not as giving as many of the members of the brotherhood are or would have outsiders believe. This energy, while not visible, is sometimes so strong and so negative that it can imprint itself onto space and time and have a future effect on the visible world.

The new brick DeLand Masonic Lodge was opened in 1925. William Carpenter, a former temple member, designed the building himself. After the brotherhood of DeLand Masons moved their meeting location to a newer lodge hall, several small businesses tried and failed to use this particular location. Many who did try to run a business within the walls claimed that there was something odd about the second floor. This happened to be the floor on which the Masons conducted their secret meetings, initiations, rituals and rites. Reports claim that there always seem to be electrical problems throughout the building, especially on the second floor. There are doors that won't stay shut, odd chanting sounds coming from upstairs and even noises of movement and footsteps when the employees or owners were on the first-floor level of the building.

When paranormal researchers finally investigated the building, all the strange occurrences were found to be true. With a normal haunting, involving a once-living human spirit or spirits and the activity associated with them, there are sometimes what is known as cold spots in areas of buildings. These cold spots are actually severe drops in temperature theorized to be the spirit or spirits using the ambient energy in the air around them to help themselves manifest in some way as to make themselves known to the living. When nonhuman spirit energy is involved in creating paranormal activity, a hot spot can sometimes be documented, the theory being that since the energy is negative in nature, it has an opposite effect on a temperature fluctuation and creates heat instead of cold. There is a documented hot spot on the second floor of the old Masonic Lodge building that moves back and forth in a very definite pattern. The hot spot begins fifteen feet to the right of where the podium still sits and moves to fifteen feet to the left of the podium. This pattern was later learned to be the same pattern or steps taken by Masonic initiates during one of their initiation rites.

There are two doors on the second floor that open by themselves even when they are shut tight and locked, as well as a sink in the men's bathroom on the second floor that continues to drip water even when the main water supply to the building itself is turned completely off. During renovations of the building, the power and water had been shut off to replace old pipes that were made of lead. The sink didn't seem to care and continued to drip water on a regular basis. Several sightings of a dark red form standing in one of the windows on the second floor have also been reported. The form is described as being cloaked with a hood covering its head and it stares down at passersby on the street in front of the building, shifting back and forth from foot to foot.

During an investigation in 2001, the owner of the building and the investigators had a frightening experience with the negative energy that resides in the old building. While standing in the middle of the floor on the second level of the building, the owner, who had been drinking a bit before allowing the investigators into the building, suddenly got on all fours and began to act in an animalistic manner. He eventually stood up and began chanting. At first, they were guttural sounds that no one could make out, but eventually he chanted in Latin, a language that he had never studied. At first it was thought that his drinking had made him act in this manner. Later, when questioned about what had occurred, the owner couldn't remember anything of what had happened. He remembered allowing the investigators into the building, standing there while they began the investigation, holding his fiancée's hand and then nothing else until he was being asked about speaking in Latin. He admitted to drinking prior to entering the building—he had had a couple of experiences in the building and was not comfortable going

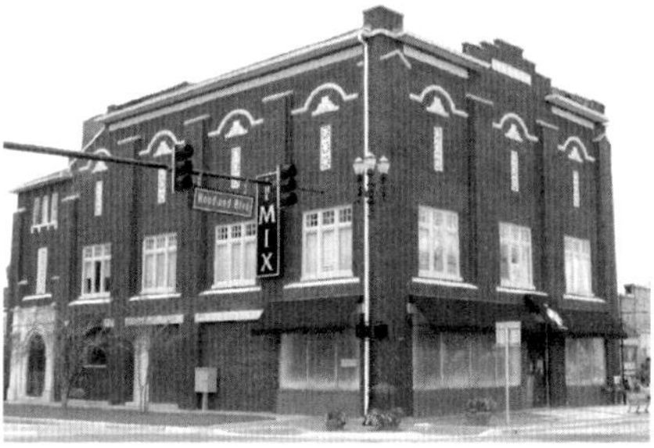

The Masonic Temple Building in 2008—still with no business on two of the three floors of the building. *Courtesy of the author.*

in even with several other people with him.

It is said by anyone who has tried and failed at running a business of any kind in the old Masonic Temple building that any business so attempted will fail. It is believed that the only way that the negative energy that resides within the walls of the building will allow another successful business is if it is reopened as another Masonic Lodge.

It is theorized by several of the researchers who were present that night that the energy created during the Masonic rituals have taken on a form of their own. This "thought-form" energy is in a sense alive in the building and is what now inhabits the second floor. Thought-forms can be created by many people believing in a similar set of values, moral codes or rules and turning them into rites and rituals. During these rites and rituals, the energy expended by the participants imprints itself onto the area and sometimes remains behind. This energy is not unlike that of a regular ghost, with the exception of the fact that they are normally negative in nature and do not like outsiders to intrude on their space. They can continue to grow long after the rites and rituals have ended if the people who performed the rites didn't close them off from the realm of the living.

This particular negative thought-form of energy appears in photos as a misshapen, dark red, cloaked and hooded figure or a thick, dark red, solid mass. It gives off heat and anyone who stands near where it is present feels hot and heavy. It gives many people who enter the building severe headaches, makes them feel nauseous and can even take them over like the old owner if they are not strong enough emotionally, psychologically or physically. It has caused many problems over the years since the original Masonic Temple closed—water leaks and other plumbing problems, electric issues such as lights turning on and off when no one is in the building—and of course all of this has affected profits of newer owners over the years. It does as it wishes and lets no one get in its way. It feels alone without the members of the Masonic Temple, and as the owner in 2001 quickly discovered, it has the ability to temporarily posses any person that stands in its way of being reunited with the energy of the rituals that created it.

Chapter 8

Sarah—the Ghost of the Old Casket Company

In 1886, a disastrous fire started in the Wilcox Saloon on what is now Woodland Boulevard in downtown DeLand. This fire was responsible for destroying a large part of DeLand and many of the original structures in the business district were lost forever. Some say that the blaze was started by people in town who were tired of the undesirable types of ruffians that frequented the saloon and caused many problems in and around town. Since these men were considered by most to be the worst kind of riffraff around, the more upstanding townsfolk felt it best to remove their gathering site. The Wilcox Saloon was doomed to become their target.

Now that DeLand had become the seat of justice for the whole of the county, this ruffian behavior and pioneer justice mentality needed to come to an end. They say the fire was never meant to harm anyone or cause any other business to suffer but intentions, whether good or bad, can't stop an enormous wall of fire. The fire caused so much damage to the wooden structures in the business district and to surrounding homes that a law was passed stating that all restored businesses would have to be made of masonry materials in the business district of DeLand. Another fire, nearly one hundred years later, would amend that law to read that *no* buildings in the business district could be made of wood.

One of the businesses to suffer complete devastation during the fire was the Casket Company. Once located in what is now the Tongue and Groove Antique Store, the Casket Company was quickly set ablaze during the Wilcox Saloon fire. Since the Casket Company's building was made of wood, and so were many of the materials contained within the building, it was a tragedy waiting to happen if a fire ever did break out.

The local blacksmith had a shop directly next door to the Casket Company, but his shop did not suffer as greatly as the Casket Company did as his materials were mostly made of iron and steel. He did lose a major part of his building, but his losses did not compare to those suffered by many others during the fire of 1886. The Casket Company tried to reopen its doors, but failed to remain in business. The financial loss due to the fire had been too great for them to recover from.

Over the years, the building has housed many businesses, from a meeting hall to a coffee shop, a bus depot and more recently an antique store now operating within the walls. When the employees and owners of the antique store first opened up their shop as Tongue and Groove Antiques, they noticed a few strange occurrences in the building. Since they had been in the antique business for many years, none of the activity struck them as being odd. Within the field of paranormal occurrences, there is an anomaly known as "possessed possessions." The basic theory behind this type of paranormal activity is that the energy from a once-living human being can imprint itself onto ordinary everyday objects and the object can retain their energy. For many people, this type of activity is well-known and experienced on a daily basis. A good example is that one of your grandparents has passed away, and you inherit their favorite rocking chair. Since you were a child, you always remembered your grandparent sitting in that chair. Now, while positioned in a place of honor and remembrance in your living room, the chair begins to rock all by itself when no one is sitting in it. This is a classic case of owning a possessed possession.

Of course, the owners of the antique store reported having the standard cold spots, a few voices and even movement of certain antique items, but the strangest thing was they seemed to know exactly who the main spirit in the store was. Anytime something otherworldly would happen, they would chuckle and say, "Oh, it was just Sarah trying to get our attention." Occasionally, when the employees would be restoring an old piece, they would get frustrated over what color would best suit the object. Sarah was always on hand to let them know, in one way or another, exactly what color she felt the piece should be. She would knock cans of stain or paint off the workroom shelves, throw fabric swatches around the room and she would even, on occasion, knock the silver polish over as if to tell the workers that they hadn't cleaned the piece of silverware good enough.

Sarah would open doors, turn lights on or off, flush toilets and even rearrange some of the antiques in stock, and she did all of this work without

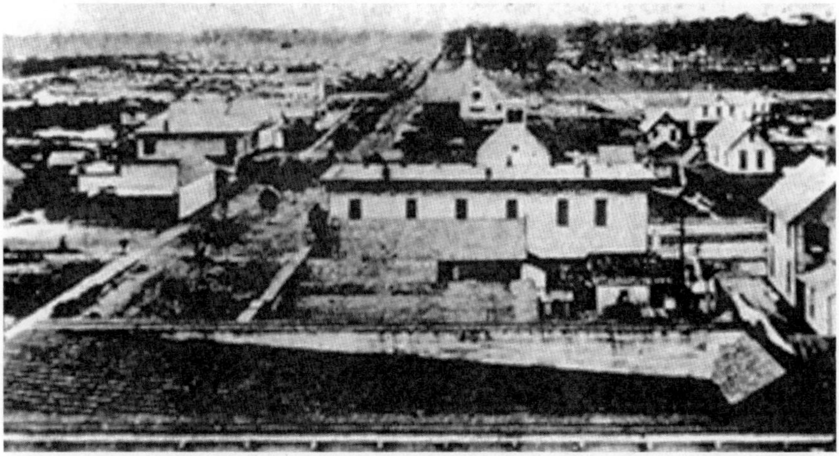

Woodland Boulevard after the devastating fires of 1886. *Courtesy of the West Volusia Historical Society.*

being asked or even being on the payroll. She is quite a helpful spirit and very well liked at the old Casket Company. But no one is really sure who she was or what time period she lived in. They don't even know if her name was really Sarah, but the female spirit seems to like being called Sarah, so the owners and employees continue to address her as such.

When the owners had a psychic called in, the clues about Sarah and who she really was seemed to narrow. The psychic claimed to have connected with Sarah and her real-life existence was dated to the early 1900s. That would be well after the fire that began at the Wilcox Saloon. It was confirmed through the psychic that her name really was Sarah, even though the psychic was never told anything about the store, the owners, employees or the spirits prior to her reading the area. Sarah was described as being in her late teens or possibly early twenties, with long, light brown hair and hazel eyes. The psychic described her as looking like a plain young woman—nothing about her made her stand out in a crowd, so to speak. She did love her father, though, and at one point the psychic began to sob and it seemed as if Sarah was speaking through her. Sarah apparently enjoyed being in the antique store, but missed her father and didn't quite understand why she never saw him there. It was then determined that Sarah's father once worked in the same building in which Sarah seems quite happy to live her afterlife. It is believed that he was a ticket salesman when the bus company was once housed in the building,

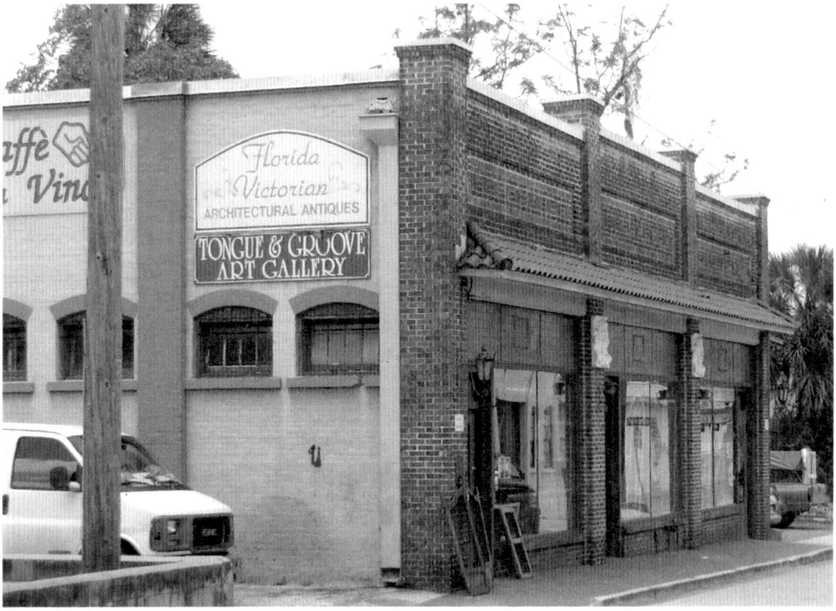

The Tongue and Groove Antique Store was once the Old Casket Company in DeLand before the fire that destroyed many downtown businesses. *Courtesy of the author.*

and when Sarah was finished with school and her chores at home for the day, she would walk to the bus depot and visit with her father until he got off work, and the two would walk back home together. When her job was completed, the psychic was told about the activity and the fact that everyone had been calling the spirit Sarah for several years. She was not surprised to hear that her psychic impressions of the building and its residents were correct.

There is also a pair of young boys' spirits that get a bit mischievous in the old Casket Company building. The employees say the boys like to play in the rafters, where the old wood is stored. Many times, employees have seen out of the corner of their eyes their little heads popping up from behind the large stacks of ancient wood. When the employees turn to get a full view of who might be playing in the somewhat dangerous stack, they find that no one is there—at least no one that is still among the living. The boys also offer cold spots, noises, set off the store's motion detectors and even open a few doors. They have even been known to play in their own spirit playground, out in the courtyard where the blacksmith's shop once stood. On many occasions, the laughter of children can be heard from the courtyard outside, but when you open the door and search the grounds no children are to be found.

One of the more interesting sightings at the old Casket Company is that of a horse-drawn hearse from the Victorian era. Before the devastating fire that brought the Casket Company to ruination, the horses and hearse were stored on the east side of the building. The destruction of the Wilcox Saloon fire consumed both the horses and the beautiful hearse they once proudly pulled—a great financial loss for the Casket Company. There have been hundreds of people who claim to hear the horses whinnying, snorting and baying on the east side of the building, especially on very hot summer nights. The horses and hearse have also been seen and photographed on a couple of occasions in their ghostly spirit state. The horses are seen black as coal with their best funeral attire proudly adorned, hitched up to the gleaming black hearse trimmed in gold with flower vases at the front, standing at the ready near where the caskets would be loaded.

Since some spirits for whatever reason choose to stay behind or even possibly get stuck behind because of sudden death, unfinished personal business, emotional or personal attachments to an area, building, person or even an item, it is no wonder that the Tongue and Groove Antique Store is chock-full of wonderful treasures from the past and from the passed away.

Chapter 9
Spirits Don't Check Out of the Artisan Inn

The DeLand Hotel, or as it is now known, the Artisan Inn, has an interesting and haunting history that began in the early 1900s. Soon after the DeLand Hotel was completed, its history of tragedies began and would not end until the late 1900s. Some of the locals believe that the land itself is tainted with negative energy that causes these tragic events to occur. But let's start at the hotel's beginning and see if we can see a pattern to the paranormal activity or if it is just merely coincidence.

In 1913, Edwin Barnhill and his wife Jeanette moved to DeLand from Grand Rapids, Michigan. They initially operated the McLeod Hotel at the corner of Florida and New York Avenues in DeLand. Later the Barnhills would also take over the management of the Atlantic Hotel in Daytona Beach. In addition to his hotel management skills, Mr. Barnhill was also well known in the area for the construction of the first open-air tour buses. These unique tourist transports were constructed by connecting two Model-T Fords together. This venture established the first bus line between DeLand and Daytona Beach.

In 1924, this local entrepreneur had a vision that rivaled Henry DeLand's vision, but with a price that most any tourist could afford without cutting the luxury aspect. Mr. Barnhill wanted to build a modest hotel for snowbirds—people traveling south to escape the long, cold Northern winters. The original building plans showed the hotel's original dimensions to be nearly twice as long as it was when the completed hotel was eventually finished. This was most likely due to a lack of funds on Mr. Barnhill's end of the construction. The Howarth family, who assumed ownership not long after completion of the project, assisted in further financing for the original DeLand Hotel.

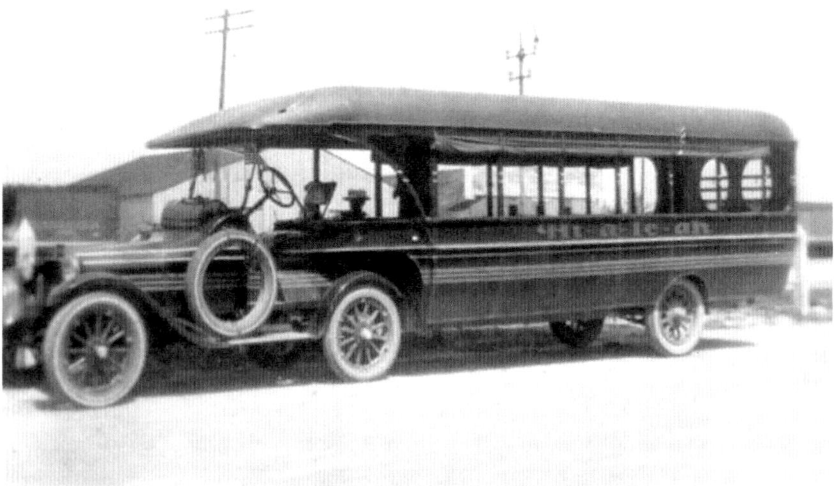

A bus similar to this one was created by Mr. Barnhill to transport tourists from DeLand to Daytona Beach. *Courtesy of the State of Florida Archives—Florida Memory Project.*

Architect Medwin Peek was hired to draft the plans for the DeLand Hotel and Andrew Bradshaw, a DeLand contractor who had earlier built the Athens Theater, supervised its construction. When the DeLand Hotel was first completed, there were more than forty individual rooms. Each room contained its own sink mounted to the wall and a closet, leaving little living space within each room and further cramping the small space provided. Two of the rooms in the hotel shared a bathroom consisting of a tub and a toilet. Amazingly enough, during that period, time sharing a bathroom with just one other room was quite a rare and special treat. Adding to the upscale luxury of the time, the building was even equipped with a fire sprinkler system. Mr. Barnhill and his wife finally opened the DeLand Hotel in February 1927.

Sadly, Jeanette Barnhill died in 1928, and Edwin was declared insane the following year. Some say his wife's spirit drove him mad. Locals of the time claimed to have heard Edwin having conversations with his wife. He would argue with her about how the DeLand Hotel should be managed, what the staff should be expected to do and what amenities should now be provided since funds were dwindling, and he would tell her to stop looking over his shoulder when he was doing the accounting for the hotel's books. Jeanette was fanatical about turning lights off when not in use as the bills for the hotel would skyrocket. Edwin had also been heard arguing with Jeanette about his drinking when she was alive—Jeanette was a teetotaler and would not allow Edwin to drink ever! Many people claim to have seen her spirit wandering the halls of the DeLand Hotel, especially on the second floor and in the bar area. When Jeanette was alive, she and Edwin had a small, modest room that they shared at the end of the hallway on the second floor.

Over the years, the hotel's clientele and condition deteriorated rapidly. During the early 1970s, only a small amount of refurbishing, upgrading and repairs were done. With the Barnhills and Howarths now out of the financial picture, the building changed hands several times to owners who were not as interested in keeping the DeLand Hotel's charm and elegance as they were at making a buck. The name of the hotel eventually changed to the Landmark Hotel in the mid-1970s and quickly began to fall into disrepair, attracting people with drug problems, alcohol addictions, low incomes and even ladies of the night. During this period, the hotel carried a seedy reputation and began renting rooms by the week, biweekly, monthly and on occasion even by the hour.

News reports circulated the story of one guest who had locked himself in his room on the second floor for several months, refusing to allow anyone in and refusing to pay his bill. He was eventually forced out by the owner with the help of local police and an eviction notice ordered by a court. There was no violent confrontation, but the squad car that arrived did sustain a slashed tire and the evictee went to jail. While being questioned, he claimed that an elderly woman told him to stay in his room and not leave. He described her as wearing clothing from the early 1920s or 1930s. The young man, whose first name coincidentally was Edwin, was declared temporarily insane and spent some time in the hospital suffering from malnutrition.

Another report claims that a young streetwalker frequently rented a small room in the Landmark Hotel to conduct business. Some say she was a young runaway trying to earn enough money to return home. Others claim she was just bad news. No matter what she was, her life was ended one night at the Landmark Hotel. She and her "guest" entered the hotel early one morning just about the time the local bars were closing. She was given a key to a room on the second floor and was not seen exiting

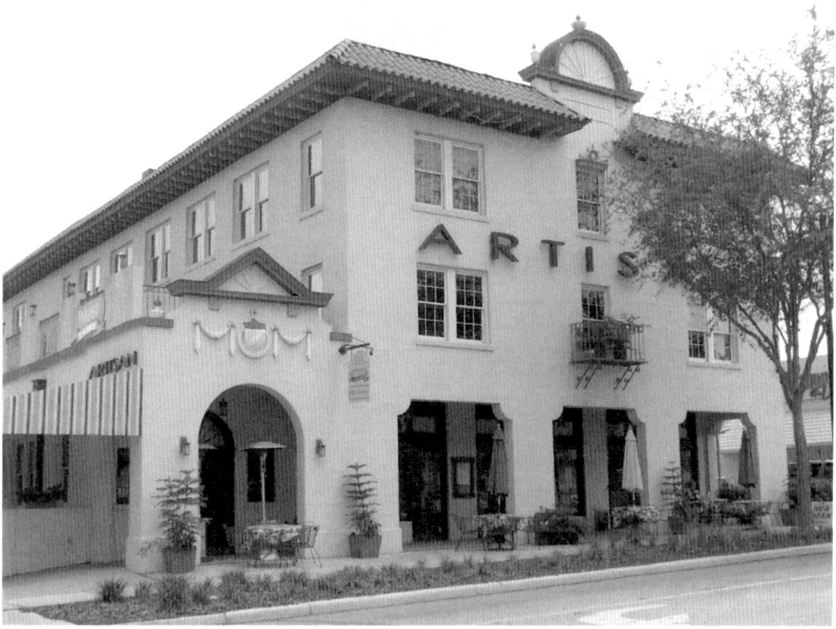

The Artisan Inn, after a full restoration, in 2008. *Courtesy of the author.*

the building with her guest as was her normal procedure. The following morning, when the manager went to get more money from her for the extra time she had spent in the room, he found her lifeless body draped over the edge of the bed, with her long hair hanging over her face. He tried to wake her only to discover that she had been strangled to death. Since no one ever paid much attention to the daily comings and goings of the various guests of the hotel, a description of her killer was never given to the police and her death remains unsolved to this day.

The hotel, while steadily degrading in both clientele and structure, remained open in some fashion until about 1985. With the hotel now becoming not only an eyesore to the beautiful downtown shopping district, but continuing to attract less and less respectable clients, a consortium of local families decided to form the Barnhill Corporation. With unknown intentions, the consortium finally purchased the building. They purchased the hotel as well as the Shell gasoline station located next door to the hotel. The Shell station was leveled and the hotel gutted of its plumbing fixtures, which were worth a small fortune, and was eventually sealed shut for nearly twelve years. Over time, many of the windows were broken out and the roof deteriorated in the harsh Florida weather, allowing water and vermin to wear away at the old structure. For years the hotel was home only to pigeons, rats, vagrants and several spirits. It was also considered to be the biggest eyesore in downtown DeLand.

During this interim of twelve years, there were many reports and sightings of what may be the spirit of Jeanette Barnhill in a window on the second floor. Locals and visitors to the area described a pale, thin woman wearing a white dress looking out the window, but no one could ever see the details of her face. Laughter and an occasional woman's scream could also be heard from time to time by people passing by on the street in front of the old decaying hotel. On the rare occasion that the authorities would be called to see if someone was trespassing, injured or worse, they found nothing. Many people just wrote the sightings off as a vagrant possibly living on the second floor, but the descriptions did and do seem to fit the description of Jeanette Barnhill.

On December 26, 1996, the old building caught the eye of two brothers who were looking for an appropriate site to set up a small restaurant business. After several months of long, hard negotiations, the Soety brothers found themselves the new owners of the Barnhill Corporation and its only asset—the rundown Landmark Hotel. The long process of restoration and alteration had begun, and some added bonuses for the new owners quickly became apparent.

It seems that a few of the mischievous spirits are longtime and permanent residents of the new Artisan Inn. One of the spirits is—as it was thought to be all along—the spirit of Jeanette Barnhill, the original owner's wife. Current employees of the establishment all say that a woman often appears in the restaurant and bar area of the Artisan Inn. This spirit has been known to toss shot glasses, break liquor bottles, move ashtrays and even turn lights on and off. She has also been seen in the elevator, which wasn't even in the building until it was restored. Sometimes, without reason, the elevator will make an unscheduled stop on the second floor. When the elevator doors open, a cold breeze blows into the elevator, and there have even been a few reports of a woman laughing and even screaming on the second floor of the Artisan Inn.

Before the hotel fell into complete abandon, a young man and his girlfriend were renting a room in the building when it was still known as the Landmark Hotel. The young man worked odd jobs for a temporary-labor service and his girlfriend worked part time as a waitress for a short while. On their evenings off, they began to frequent a local and popular nightclub located in the bottom floor of another local hotel named the Putnam Hotel. Before they knew it, their drinking habit, and another habit that involved illegal drugs, started taking control of their lives. The meager combined income of the young couple was not enough to keep their rent and new habits going. As their drug habit escalated, so did the debt they now owed to the drug dealer. The couple was found dead one morning. They had both obviously been doing large quantities of drugs and overdosed together. No one is quite sure if they purposefully overdosed or not—only the young couple knows for sure. They were lovingly holding one another in bed in their modest run-down room at the Landmark Hotel. People who visit that area of the restored Artisan Inn say there is always an eerie, cold area in the room right in the spot were the young couple's bed once was and where they were found dead in love's embrace.

Whoever the spirits are that still reside in the Artisan Inn, one thing is for sure—they are very active, very interactive and will remain residents until the end of time.

Chapter 10
Footsteps and Spirits in the Fernery

During the Civil War, the state of Florida was not as ravaged as several other Southern states were. After all, there were no decisive battles that were fought on Florida soil. While Union forces occupied many coastal towns and forts, the interior of the state remained in Confederate hands. There were several troops stationed at small forts throughout the DeLand area at the time and many lives were changed for the worse, even though they did not see the horrors of war on such battlefields as Gettysburg.

Florida provided an estimated fifteen thousand troops and significant amounts of supplies, including salt, beef, pork, turpentine and cotton, to the Confederacy; more than two thousand Floridians, both African American and white, joined the Union Army. Confederate and foreign merchant ships would slip through the Union Navy blockade along the coast, bringing needed supplies from overseas ports.

Tallahassee was the only Southern capital east of the Mississippi River to avoid capture during the war, spared by Southern victories at Olustee in 1864 and Natural Bridge in 1865. Ultimately, the South was defeated and Federal troops occupied Tallahassee on May 10, 1865.

Before the Civil War, Florida was well on its way to becoming another of the Southern states to produce cotton. After the war, the lives of many residents changed. When it finally ended, the ports of Jacksonville and Pensacola again flourished due to the demand for lumber products to rebuild the nation's cities that had been so severely damaged and those that were almost totally destroyed. Those who had been slaves were at last declared free. Plantation owners tried to regain prewar levels of production

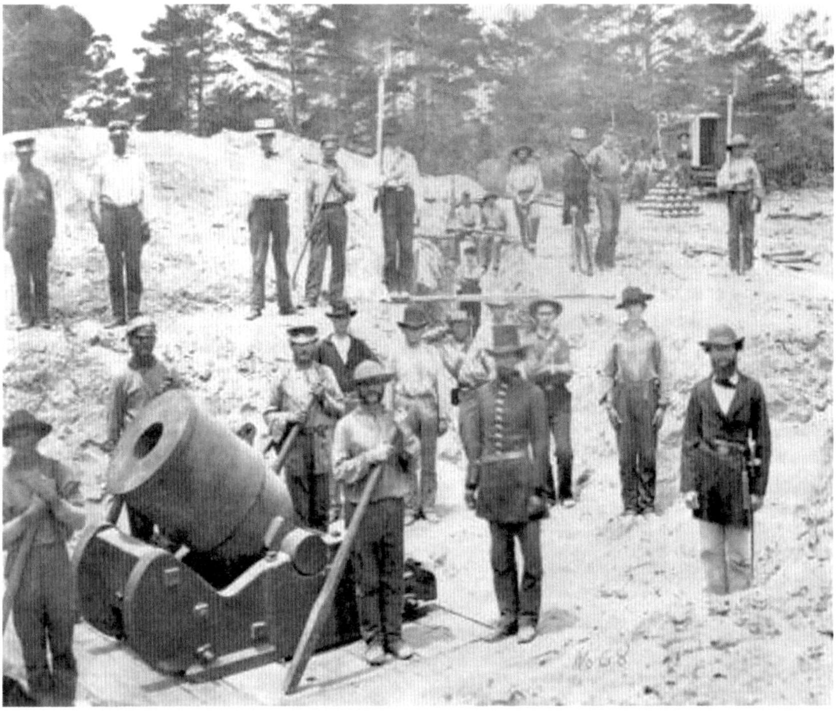

Civil War soldiers in Florida. *Courtesy of the State of Florida Archives—Florida Memory Project.*

by hiring former slaves to raise and pick cotton. However, such programs did not work well, and much of the land came under cultivation by tenant farmers and sharecroppers, both African American and white.

Before the war began, an African American slave woman named Ruby worked on a small cotton plantation on the northern end of what is now the DeLand–DeLeon Springs border. Ruby was a hard worker and worked alongside many of her own family members, including her aunt Charity. Ruby and Charity were very close. Ruby's mother had died giving birth to her younger sister, and Ruby's aunt Charity had become her surrogate mother. The two talked about everything together—the future, life, the mysteries of the universe and how a young man who also worked on the cotton plantation had taken a fancy to young Ruby.

It seems that Ruby's hard work caught the eye of the plantation owner as well as the eye of one of his young white foremen. Ruby noticed the young man's flirtatious behavior when they would work long days together, but she tried to pay no attention to the young man as she tried to focus on her work. She did, however, appreciate his kindness. He would give Ruby a few extra minutes on breaks, give her fresh, cool water before anyone else and would even sometimes give her extra food from his own plate at meal time. Back then these things simply were not done between whites and blacks.

When the war began, Ruby's life changed drastically, like so many others. Her family members were ripped apart and hidden throughout the state of Florida. The only family member that she knew the whereabouts of was her aunt. It seems her aunt Charity was hidden away in swamps by Confederate soldiers in Jefferson County and forced to make soap for them. When the war ended, Charity returned to her owners' plantation, where she lived until they died. Charity and Ruby were never reunited.

Ruby's life remained relatively normal during the Civil War. She stayed in the DeLand area and worked in the same fields as before the war began. The young foreman who had taken a shine to Ruby didn't stay behind. He joined the Confederate forces and went off to war late in the game. While Ruby knew it was wrong, she couldn't help but think about the young foreman and she dreamed of when they might be together again. She missed the special treatment he would kindly give her and hoped he would return home one day alive and well. With so many reports of captured soldiers, the horrors of Northern winters and even death, she feared for his life like any woman would do when "her" man went off to war.

The cotton plantation also succumbed to the ravages of war. The plantation owner couldn't keep up with getting seeds delivered on time, which put planting behind, and with the many slaves now signing up to serve in the military, he didn't have the workforce he once had to keep the crop coming in on time. Now with her future and her job about to fade into the void of despair, Ruby fell into an emotional depression. She missed her family, her friends, her former coworkers and her foreman. She dreaded getting out of bed each day and now hated picking the crop she once enjoyed working. At her very young age she felt that her life was at an end.

The war eventually ended and in 1868, the federal government instituted a congressional program of reconstruction in Florida and the other Southern states. During this time period, Republican officeholders tried to enact sweeping changes, many of which were aimed at improving conditions for African Americans. At the time of the 1876 presidential election, Federal troops were still occupying Florida. The state's Republican government and recently enfranchised African American

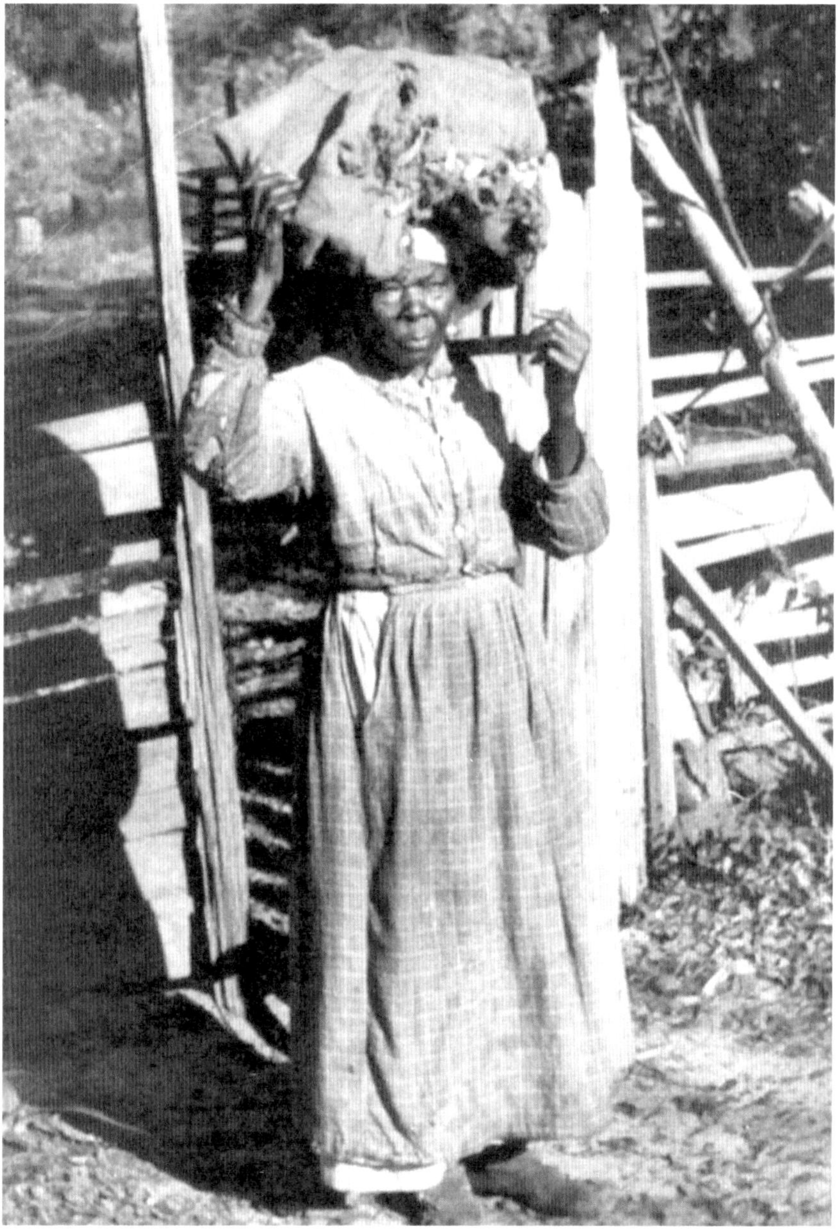

Charity Stewart was ninety-three years old when this photo was taken in 1937. *Courtesy of the State of Florida Archives—Florida Memory Project.*

voters helped to put Rutherford B. Hayes in the White House. However, Democrats gained control of enough state offices to end the years of Republican rule and prompt the removal of Federal troops the following year. A series of political battles in the state again left African Americans with little voice in their government.

While all of this mattered to some newly freed African Americans, some, like Ruby, didn't care. All she knew was that she was now free and had no job, nowhere to live, no family she could find and had no news of her foreman. Voting for a president had no meaning to poor Ruby, neither did the fact that she was now free. For Ruby, it was something akin to what many modern prisoners face after long terms of incarceration. While the thought of being out of their cage is appealing, when they finally make it to the outside world and true freedom, they have no idea how to live their own lives. On the inside, life is structured and they are told exactly what to do and how to do it for every minute of their day. Once on the outside, fear grips them and some even return to a life of crime to go back to the familiarity of prison. This is the same thing that Ruby now faced—fear!

Ruby finally found work at a fernery near the old cotton plantation. Cotton was quickly being replaced by this commercial crop in Florida and there were plenty of new jobs available. While the pay wasn't very good, there was a small compensatory communal living facility on the grounds, meals were included and she did get one afternoon a week off. Things had started to look up for Ruby and she now looked at the future with a somewhat-brighter outlook than before. Although she still had no word of her foreman and it was now several years after the war had ended, she had given up hope that he would ever return.

On one of her afternoons off, Ruby was lying under an oak tree at the southern end of the fernery when she noticed a man coming toward her. The position of the sun kept her from clearly seeing his face until he was right in front of her. She looked up and shielded her eyes with her hand at her brow and was amazed to see the young foreman. He was still wearing his uniform, as it was the only clothing he possessed at the time. He had survived the war and returned to the area in search of work. He smiled widely at her and told her how he had kept her in his thoughts all these years—she was what got him through the war and he felt he had someone to return home to. Ruby blushed with delight and offered the young man a seat next to her under the oak tree.

Her freedom from slavery also meant she now had the freedom to pursue his affections if she chose to. She listened intently to every word

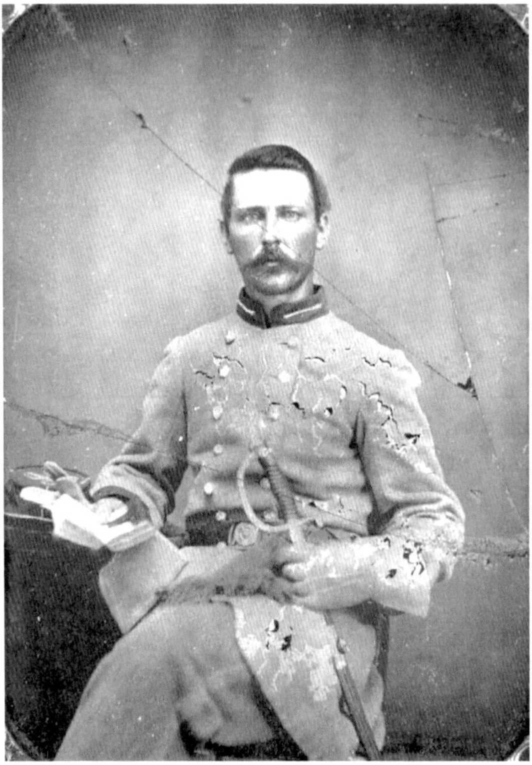

Claimed to be a portrait taken of Joshua during his service in the Civil War. *Courtesy of the State of Florida Archives—Florida Memory Project.*

he said and shed a tear when he told her of how he watched a close friend of his die on the battlefield. He gently wiped away her tear and that was the moment she knew she was in love with him. He leaned over and kissed her sweetly on the cheek and said, "I know this is kind of sudden, but, will you marry me?" Ruby's mouth dropped open and her eyes got wider. She thought for only a moment and replied, "Yes, I will marry you."

He explained that he had little money but that he wanted their life together to be as happy as it could be. He would apply for work at the same fernery she worked at and tell his future employer that he could begin right after their wedding. He told her that he knew of a nice place to honeymoon for a couple of days over in Monroe County, only a five-day ride by horseback, and they could be married there as well. Ruby giggled with glee and agreed that anything he wanted would be fine with her. Her mind began racing with thoughts of their wedding day and how their lives would be once they returned to DeLand. Ruby's life had changed again, this time for the better.

The couple rode off early the following morning and headed for Monroe County. The groom-to-be had secured the job he inquired about and he knew their lives would be wonderful once they got started. His new employer also gave him a set of clothing. He told him that there were still Yankees in the state and he might be arrested or shot on sight, but thanked him for his service to the South and said that the South would rise again. The soldier thanked his new employer and turned his attention back to the task of the day and to his charming and beautiful bride-to-be. Their employer's wife also leant Ruby a beautiful white dress to be married in. The young couple talked for most of the ride and learned that they had a great deal in common. They both wanted lots of children as both of them had come from large families, and neither could see any reason to stop a family tradition, so to speak. They both hoped the first would be a boy and wanted to name him Joshua, after his soon-to-be father. They also discussed the possibilities of sharecropping or even some day owning their own plantation for either ferns, cotton, turpentine, honey or maybe even citrus. During part of their journey, Joshua played on his mouth harp, an instrument he learned to play while serving in the army. Ruby enjoyed his music and even sang along for some of the songs she knew. The days flew by and before they knew it, they had arrived at their destination.

The next morning, they woke early and headed straight for the Monroe County Courthouse. They both stood nervously on the steps until the door was unlocked and opened. Joshua stated their intentions for marriage and the clerk escorted the couple to the judge's chamber door. Judge James Dean, who was elected over two white candidates and was said to be the first African American judge to be elected after Reconstruction in Florida, was to preside over their nuptials. Judge Dean asked if Ruby was African American—he felt it might damage his career if certain officials found out he married a white man to a black woman and was told by Joshua that she was mulatto. Ruby squeezed his hand hard but kept quiet as she wanted to marry her beau. Judge Dean was later removed from his office for marrying the couple by Governor Francis P. Fleming, but in 2002, his judgeship was reinstated by Governor Jeb Bush—a little too late, as Judge Dean married the couple in 1888.

The ceremony went off without a hitch and the couple kissed in a deep, loving embrace for the first time since they had met nearly two decades ago. The clerk threw some torn-up paper at them as they headed out the door with the marriage certificate in hand. They spent two leisurely

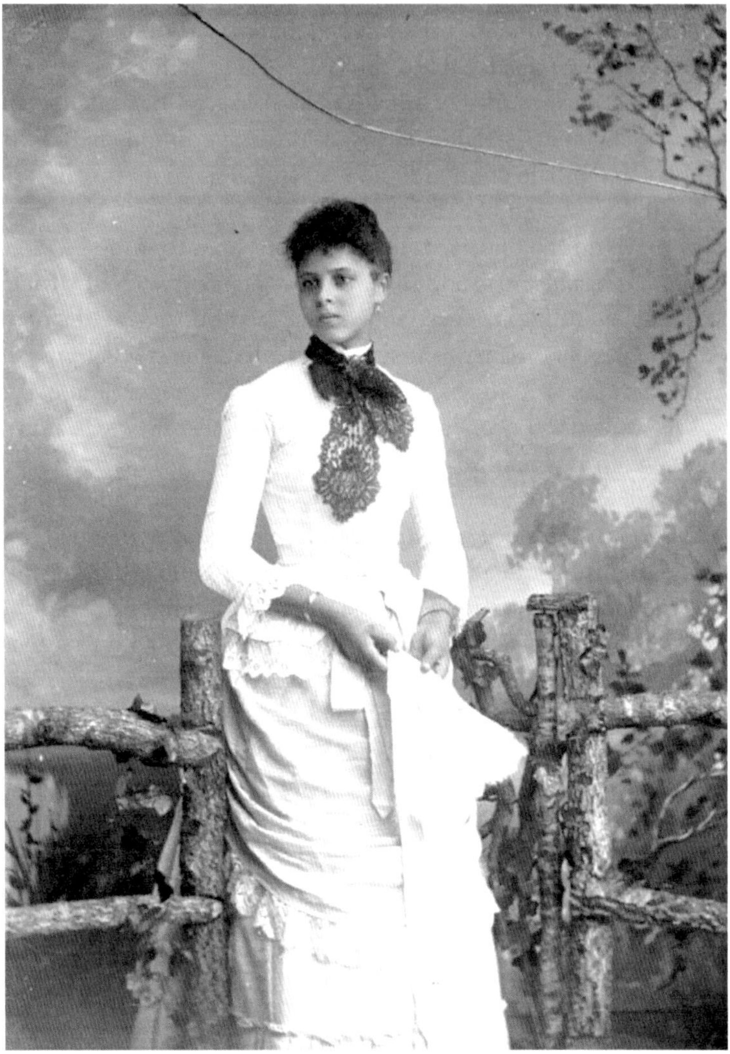

This is said to be a photo of Ruby on her wedding day. *Courtesy of the State of Florida Archives—Florida Memory Project.*

days honeymooning, embraced in one another's arms, and then packed up to ride home to Volusia County and to their lives together. They both now looked forward to working, buying their own place to live, having children and maybe eventually getting their own land to raise crops on. They discussed all the possibilities of their new lives together on their journey home and Ruby commented that she hoped the stork would visit in nine months—call it mother's intuition, or maybe she was psychic, but nine months to the day after the first night of their honeymoon Joshua Jr. was born!

While to this day some Southerners believe that slavery should still exist, most do not. In Ruby and Joshua's day, most did. Their employer didn't care either way—they were both good, hard workers, even though Ruby was pregnant, and he saw past the color barrier to the love the young couple had for each other. Some of their coworkers were not so colorblind. Soon after they returned from their honeymoon, rumors began to circulate about "taking care" of the situation.

Ruby and Joshua slept in separate quarters at the fernery. Many of the women that shared the small space with Ruby wouldn't even speak to her. The same held true for the men in the housing quarters that Joshua slept in. With the exception of the occasional joke made at Ruby's expense, Joshua kept his tongue and didn't let their rude comments bother him. He knew what a good woman Ruby was and her skin color had nothing to do with how he felt about her. He knew it was silly and narrow-minded of these men to think the way they did, but after all this was a free country and they were entitled to their opinion, right? Joshua didn't like his coworker Isaac's wife—she was fat, lazy and smelled something awful, but he never brought that subject up. Both Ruby and Joshua worked longer hours, getting up earlier than the rest of the workers and staying in the fields later, just to avoid more comments and any ridiculous confrontations that might occur.

This plan worked very well until the final month of Ruby's pregnancy. Ruby had hidden her pregnancy well until that time by wearing oversized clothing and keeping her back to coworkers whenever she could. She bathed alone and never undressed in front of her roommates. When she could no longer hide her ever-growing girth, the ridicule, jokes and threats worsened. Her employer felt that for her safety, as well as the safety of the unborn baby, Ruby should change her job description temporarily and work at his private home. Ruby and Joshua agreed and were thankful for his understanding. This would also give the couple short bits of time to spend together alone in the evenings after work.

Ruby stayed at her employer's home for three months after the baby was born. It was then that she decided that she would return to the housing on the fernery property and stand up for herself, her baby and her husband if anyone had anything to say about it. Poor Ruby had no idea what this choice would set into motion. From the moment she returned, the ridicule began. She knew she was strong emotionally and could ignore their silly verbal comments, but when she began to find small dead animals in her bunk, she started to worry. At first, she didn't mention this fact to Joshua or her employer—she didn't want to make things worse or go back to living somewhere else. She hoped it would stop or that Joshua would save enough money for them to get their own place. She decided it was time to make plans to speak with him after work one day.

During one of their breaks, Ruby walked over to where the men were standing and asked to speak with her husband privately. The other men laughed and made rude comments about both Ruby and Joshua Jr. Joshua worked his way through the crowd of men and walked his wife a few steps away and the couple embraced. They began to speak of moving and finding a place of their own when the men started making louder and louder comments. They became so loud that the couple finally decided to hold this conversation off until Sunday, two days away, until they could have some privacy. They would meet under the oak tree where Joshua had proposed to Ruby at sunset.

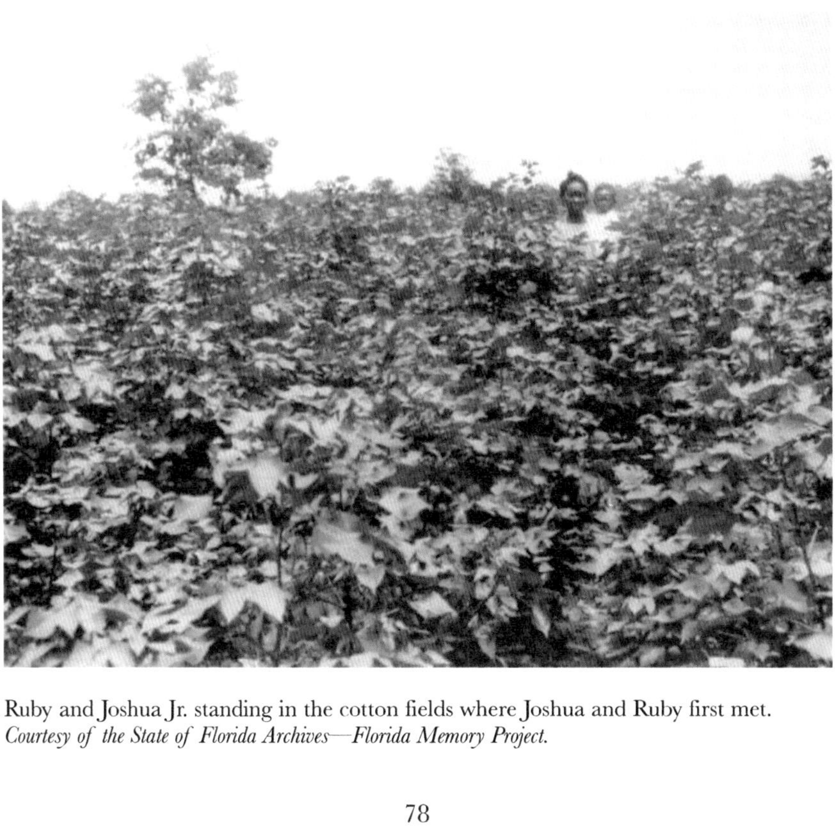

Ruby and Joshua Jr. standing in the cotton fields where Joshua and Ruby first met. *Courtesy of the State of Florida Archives—Florida Memory Project.*

Sunday came and Ruby waited patiently for the meeting with her husband. Just before sunset, she headed out of the shack toward the oak tree with their baby tied in a sash at her waist. As she walked across the dusty dirt trails that cut through the fernery, she noticed several of the men standing around and shooting her nasty looks, but none of them made any rude comments as was now the norm. She quickened her pace as the sky turned to hues of burnt orange and purple, nervous and curious as to why the other male workers were acting so strangely. She also realized that none of the women in her shack were speaking when she left. They were all just sitting around, quietly staring at the floor, wall or out the small window. Her mother's intuition kicked in again and thoughts began to race through her mind that something was very wrong with Joshua.

When she arrived at the oak tree, she didn't see Joshua. Her heart raced and she felt sick. She knew something was wrong, but couldn't place what it was. The oak tree was very large and she thought to herself that maybe Joshua was around the other side of the trunk. Ruby circled the tree and still didn't find her husband. She heard footsteps coming from behind her and breathed a sigh of relief as she turned to see her love. She stopped mid-smile when she saw several of the male workers standing behind her. Ruby gripped her baby tight to her chest and as she started to ask what they wanted one of the men simply pointed up. Ruby looked back at the man, confused, and then realized that he wanted her to look up. She almost couldn't bring herself to do it. She knew something was terribly wrong. She finally glanced up and, for that split second, saw only the bottom of a man's boots. She fell to the ground, weeping incessantly; she knew at that moment these men had taken her husband's life by hanging him in that oak tree.

It was then that Ruby's employer came to the scene. He told the other workers to get back to their shacks or leave for good. Some stayed and some left stating that anyone who condoned blacks and whites being together and "breeding" wasn't worth working for. He and his wife cared for Ruby and they took her and the baby back to their home, where Ruby stayed in shock for several weeks. He also cut Joshua down from the tree and buried him at its base. He brought Ruby to visit Joshua every day, but she never recovered from her loss. Ruby felt that it was her fault that the men had killed her love. If she would have stayed at the main house this never would have happened to him.

Her employer also pseudoadopted Joshua Jr. and raised him as one of his own; since Ruby lost Joshua, she was unable to care for her infant, nor did she want to. Just three short months after Joshua was so brutally murdered, Ruby took her own life at the base of the oak tree, right next to Joshua's grave site. She simply ate a large amount of poisonous oleander flowers and lay down beside Joshua and went to sleep, never to wake again.

Time has gone by quickly at the old fernery. It remained in the family, open and producing ferns for many years, but finally closed for business in the early 1980s. It now sits abandoned, with ferns growing wild and plenty of native wildlife now taking up residence. Many people live around the outside of the property border and even walk through it in the cool of the evening to walk off dinner or walk their dog, while some use it as a quicker route through the neighborhood. It is a quiet place away from the hustle and bustle of town, except at night, especially when eerie dense fog rolls in. It is at this time that the serenity of the abandoned fernery will send chills down your spine.

There have been hundreds of sightings at the fernery of a young man dressed in a Civil War Confederate soldier's uniform, standing at the center of the field that leads to the old oak tree. He has also been seen standing and sometimes sitting at the base of the oak tree, where Joshua proposed to Ruby all those years ago. There have also been sightings, photographs and reports of a man hanging from one of the high branches in that same old oak tree. Music is also heard in the fernery, music that comes from a mouth harp. What is believed to be Ruby's spirit is also seen in the fernery. She stands by the base of the old oak tree, is seen walking the dirt driveways that meander through the fields and is seen by where the old shack she once lived in used to stand.

One of the eeriest experiences one can have at the old fernery is when you quietly walk through on dark, foggy nights from where that shack once stood, down the dusty dirt roads to the base of the old oak tree. You will always hear footsteps coming from behind you. When you turn to see if someone or some animal is behind you, there is never anyone or anything there. However, once you make it to the oak tree, the footsteps stop and leaves will fall from the high branch from which Joshua was hung and lost his life all those years ago.

Chapter 11
Roy Cook and the KKK

The following chapter is in no way meant to upset or degrade anyone. Nor is it meant to encourage, promote, endorse or approve of the social—or as some of them believe, religious—group that Mr. Roy Cook or anyone else chose to make a part of their lives. I do understand that bigotry is a part of our history and is sometimes present today. This great nation we live in has laws that allow people of all walks of life a chance to embrace many different types of religions, social and cultural aspects and freedoms that some do not or will not try to understand. Please remember while reading this chapter that this is a part of U.S. history, whether we like it or not, and we should learn from the mistakes as well as triumphs of others. Or, more simply put, all that we've learned from our history is that we don't learn from our history. You may find by reading on that there is a very different aspect of this certain group that you may not have realized, and you may not have known that this aspect has been changed over the years and the original message has gotten lost in time. There are also some photos that some may find disturbing. These are the facts of our history—they are not included in this work for shock value but for historical value.

Over my many years of doing cemetery preservation and restoration work, I have seen many disturbing things in the way of vandalism. Personal mementos, war medals, jewelry and even body parts stolen out of graves that have been broken into. I will never understand these things. When I first saw the headstone of Roy Cook, I was shocked. How could someone so blatantly place "KKK" and a flaming cross on their headstone? Then it hit me—it was his pride. Roy Cook was proud to be a member of the KKK. Just as you or I might place a fraternal organization or special symbol on our own headstone, so did Roy Cook. What now bothers me about his headstone is that so many people don't understand what the KKK was all about in its infancy. They know what they know of it from this century, and many ignorant people have tried to deface Roy Cook's headstone. This should never happen! They carve, spray paint or write with indelible marker obscenities onto this privately owned sculpture. Yes, folks—a headstone is a privately owned sculpture and is not to be touched by anyone except the owner or the owner's family. No matter what one's personal beliefs are, their final resting place should remain undisturbed. That is why it is a final *resting* place.

While slavery has been a part of every culture throughout the millennia, it has never been as degrading as it was for African Americans when they were ripped from their homes and forcibly brought to the New World. Many cultures treated their slaves like family members; some of them even gave them their family name. This was the case here in the New World for some luckier slaves. Not all of them were this lucky. Some were treated terribly. They were made to work long hours under bad conditions, given only enough food to sustain them, they were beaten and raped and some were even killed for a myriad of reasons, many of which would make no sense to a thinking person in a modern culture.

My father used to say, "The problems in America today are: the English language, education, lousy parenting skills and lazy people. There are whites and white trash, Puerto Ricans and spics, Chinese and chinks, Mexicans and wetbacks, blacks and n***ers. The problem is that no word in the English language has the impact on any one specific cultural group of people that the 'n-word' has. You can call a white guy a cracker or white trash all day long and he won't care, but call a black person by the 'n-word' and you can start a riot. Our schools don't educate the children with morals anymore; both parents have to work to pay all the bills so the kids are off on their own doing who knows what, and people have just gotten plain old lazy with all the new technology we have available today." My father died in 1979. I'm relatively sure he is turning in his grave at how the world has worsened. While my father's words were harsh, he was right, but he was also a bigot. I learned through both his insight and ignorance how I didn't want to be as an adult, like most kids hope they won't be like their parents.

When slavery was abolished in America, African Americans were promised several things by the president. They were told that they would get a mule, an acre of land and money to begin their new lives. This, of course, never happened. I've heard many arguments over the years that some feel this is still owed to the black populous of America, but let's face it folks—what would you do with a mule today? My ancestors were immigrants—they, of course, weren't forcibly brought here—but they lived almost like slaves early on. They endured lousy living conditions, worked like slaves, were paid very little, were beaten if they didn't do their jobs and ate nothing but potatoes for a long time. They moved forward and got over it.

In a radio talk show interview that I heard several years ago, a man had done a study and found that if the U.S. government took all the money they spent on welfare, Medicaid and food stamp programs in one year and spent it on just African Americans, they could send half of all of the African Americans living in America back to Africa. At that point, the talk show host commented that instead of sending half of them all the way back, we should send all of them half-way back. He was fired from his job immediately—this is exactly the narrow-minded mentality that still survives in some places in the Southern states and is taught by the modern Ku Klux Klan.

With all of the above stated, keep an open mind as you read on and try to understand what life was like in the late 1800s in America, specifically central Florida and specifically for a young white man growing up in the new South.

The original Ku Klux Klan as a single, united group existed from the beginning of the Civil War until it was officially ended in 1877. While today's modern KKK groups are fighting for a goal that is a far cry from what the original KKK fought for, it is believed that if you have a better understanding of exactly what was going on during the Reconstruction, just about any race of man today would have joined such a group if put in their shoes. It had a purpose, and it came out to fight for it. Once the job was done, the group closed up shop. KKK groups today have no such purpose as they did back then, and their actions today have different intentions and outcomes.

Try to imagine yourself living in the South in the late 1860s. The Yankees have invaded, and have gone across the land stealing and destroying nearly all of your family's belongings. They are digging up graves for treasured items such as jewelry, gold teeth, war medals, bronze and brass fixtures and other mementos. Many of these ruthless Yankees have raped and killed your wives, daughters and slaves. They have poured oil all over your fields so you will be unable to grow crops for many years. They have stolen every sign of food in the area, and they have taken away everything that is dear to you. They have burned down your home, barns and other outbuildings, and have left you literally out in the cold. You must now try to get back your life.

If all of this wasn't bad enough, you now find that all sense of state government has been destroyed and replaced by armed soldiers in and around your neighborhoods and in your homes and they are strictly forcing their views upon you. They come and go as they please, continuing to abuse you and your family and continuing to sexually abuse your wife, daughters and whatever freed slaves you may have left working for you—which are now few and far between. They will not allow any white Southerner to vote for anything. Voting is granted only to the uneducated former slaves, who have now been forced to make it on their own, and they are only allowed to vote if they vote for the party in charge. An example of how they were to vote is found on one of the official banners displayed in Georgia voting booths during the 1868 presidential campaign: "Every man [Negro] that didn't vote the Radical [Republican] ticket, this is the way we want to serve him: hang him by the neck." If they refuse, they are abused and even killed. Essentially, the voting process is just a farce, as you now have no choice but the choice you are given.

On top of all of this, you have scalawags and carpetbaggers coming down and holding secret meeting, teaching the freed slaves the best ways to go back and take vengeance on their former masters. They are armed and taught how to kill, rape or destroy anyone or anything they can, and then sent out in the night to do so. On top of Yankee atrocities already having taken place, you now have this rebellion going on behind the scenes. Masses of former slaves are going out raping, killing, burning and destroying whatever comes across their path—the torture continues well after the war.

Northern troops now begin flooding into the South and these men carry with them very hostile ideas and ideals. They bring heavy taxation and more abuse. Along with them comes the Union League, supported by a new militia of black Union soldiers. They move right into the plantations, cities, towns and villages, looking for the former slaves. The illiterate, simple-minded, newly freed men become easy prey for their political agenda—hate the whites, hate your masters and vote for us; we will divide the spoils of the South with you. The Union League and militia constantly insult the whites in front of the former slaves, giving them the illusion that they have great power and superiority. By telling them they would soon acquire the land of their former masters, these newly freed black men have false expectations and are furnished with a disincentive to find *real* work.

Secret clubs are established with the intent of raising the former slaves into political power over the Southern whites. It almost soon becomes "anything goes," with the former slaves abusing and threatening whites at every turn, causing the beaten-down Southern whites to live in much fear. The Union League, militia and former slaves patrol the streets, harassing and threatening everyone, especially the wives and daughters in these towns.

In the beginning, the Ku Klux Klan was organized by a small group of men to have fun and provide some "comic relief" for their beaten-down families and neighbors. On December 24, 1865, at Pulaski, Tennessee, during a meeting in a small law office, Captain John C. Lester said, "Boys, let's start something to break this monotony, and to cheer up our mothers and the girls. Let's start a club of some kind."

During this evening, the organization was perfected. Captain John B. Kennedy, on the committee to select a name, mentioned one that he had considered—"kukloi," from the Greek word "kuklos," meaning a band or circle. James R. Crowe said, "Call us the Ku Klux," and no one will know what it means. John C. Lester said, "Add Klan as we are all Scotch-Irish descent." He then repeated the words, "Ku Klux Klan." This was the first time these words were ever heard by a human ear. The weirdness of the alliteration appealed to the mysterious nature within them. The name was adopted with an inherent feeling that they had chosen something that would excite the curiosity of their friends and carry out their idea of amusement, which most unexpectedly to them proved a boon to Pulaski and the South.

James C. Crowe suggested the adoption of a costume to make the idea more mysterious. They then made a raid upon Mrs. Martin's linen closet and robed themselves with boyish glee in her stiff linen sheets and pillow cases—masquerading was a popular form of entertainment in those days. Wishing to make an impression, they borrowed some horses from a nearby stable and disguised them with sheets as well. They then mounted and rode through the darkness, calling upon the homes of their mothers and sweethearts without speaking a word. They rode slowly through the streets of Pulaski, waving to the people and making grotesque gestures that brought merriment to those in the community who were not superstitious and brought great fear to those who were.

The spirits of the people were greatly beaten-down after the war and especially during Reconstruction, and it was a very sad state of affairs. These ex-soldiers created homemade costumes and rode through town like clowns, making faces and acting as silly as they could and wanted to. However, they noticed that many former slaves saw these strange horseman and thought that they were the ghosts of the Confederate dead. This caused many rebellious former slaves to cease their destructive and lawless activities and return to seeking gainful employment.

Charles Francis Adams, the grandson of John Quincy Adams, once stated:

> *I have ever been one of those who have thought extremely severe measures were dealt the Southern people after the Civil War, measures of unprecedented severity. The Southern community was not only desolated during the war, but $3,000,000,000 of property confiscated after the war. I am not aware that history records a similar act super-added to the destruction and desolation of war.*
>
> *Their manumitted slaves belonging to an inferior and alien race, were enfranchised and put in control of the whole administration. Is there a similar case recorded in history? If so I have never heard of it. It was simply a case of insane procedure, and naturally resulted in disaster. We stabbed the South to the quick, and during all the years of Reconstruction turned the dagger round and round in the festering wound. If the South had been permitted to leave, slavery would have died a natural death.*

In the face of the overwhelming abuse and oppression placed upon them, it is not hard to understand how this costumed farce soon became a tool to be used to restore the order and balance once in place. It was at this time that the Ku Klux Klan turned from a fun-loving group of men trying to lighten the lives of their friends, neighbors and loved ones into a militant group with the purpose to preserve white rule in the South and to protect themselves from militant former slaves, who now sought out revenge at any cost.

The Ku Klux Klan soon developed a system that allowed them to monitor the secret meetings and rallies that the carpetbaggers and Union League soldiers were holding with the former slaves. The Klan would rally men and horses in full costume and ride through, breaking up these meetings that were meant to teach and incite rebellion and destruction. In a sense, these men became a form of the law, since rarely was a crime against a white punished under this new regime. When men of *any* color were caught destroying property, raping or committing any crime, they were dealt with by the KKK. It was not as if the Ku Klux Klan simply rode around town looking for any and every black man to lynch or kill—it was seeking the rebellious, destructive ones and restoring order to the chaos wherever and whenever possible.

The Ku Klux Klan was greatly opposed to the shedding of human blood, and violence was never used except as an absolute last resort. Repeated warnings were given to offenders, and it was only when these warnings were not heeded that the Ku Klux Klan resorted to extreme measures. Its methods were generally peaceful and abhorred the destruction of life or property, and when its objectives had been accomplished, no one was further persecuted or hounded and no more property was further pillaged. When peace and tranquility were restored to the land, the Ku Klux Klan folded their tents and silently stole away into the night, so to speak.

In *Secret Political Societies in the South During the Period of Reconstruction*, Walter Henry Cook, a distant relative of Roy Cook and graduate of Western Reserve University in Cleveland, Ohio, writes:

> *The Ku Klux Klan accomplished much. From a political viewpoint it secured home rule for several of the Southern States; it ended the disgraceful rule of the carpetbaggers therein; and it helped to re-establish honest and efficient governmental institutions. This example was an inspiration which after 1872 soon led the men of the Southern States still in Radical control to a glorious victory in regaining self-government. From an economic standpoint, the negroes had been frightened into going to work, and were prevented to a large extent, from breaking labor contracts. These were important services in the rehabilitation of the South. From a social standpoint the Klan had protected property, had protected life, and had brought order out of chaos.*
>
> *Given the circumstances and abuse that came down on the Southern Whites at the hand of Northerners and blacks after the war, you will hopefully understand the meaning of the olde South when they referred to "white supremacy." They sought to preserve their culture and land. It did not necessarily have reference to a hatred of blacks by the whites, but simply the restoration or order as it was, with the whites regaining the political power, as they once had, in maintaining the peace in the political realm. You have to stop thinking like a 21st Century person, and remember*

> *that back then, the negro race was not as educated as today. They were not always as fit for political leadership, etc. as the educated European white race had been for centuries. This view of white supremacy was strongly held in both regions, North and South, so it was not a "Southern thang." I believe that any race, put into the shoes of the white men after the war, would cry for supremacy of their race, and most likely seek to protect their homes, families and land in a similar manner as the Klan did.*

During Reconstruction, the lawlessness started at the top of the governmental food chain and worked its way down to the bottom of the gutter. Louisiana Governor Waymouth accumulated $1.5 million in only four years and on a salary of $8,000 a year. The newly self-elected carpetbagger government of Florida saw fit to steal meat and flour slatted to be given to helpless women and children. In North Carolina, newly freed slave convicts were made justices of the peace and these men were unable to read or write! A similar situation was going on in South Carolina, where ninety-four black men were appointed to the legislature as speaker of the house, clerk of the house, door keeper, chairman of the Ways and Means Committee and the chaplain—some of these men could neither read nor write either.

After all of this—a terrible war, slavery, carpetbagger governments, bribery, rape, pillaging and far worse—how would you react? Try to envision yourself in earlier scenarios, such as found in films like *Braveheart* and *The Patriot*, two films that may give you some sort of understanding of how it was at those times. In each of these films, you have tyrannical soldiers monitoring your every move, starving your families, burning your homes, stealing what they wanted, abusing your women and harassing the people in general. There was physical and sexual abuse, no one was allowed to question the ruling government and anyone who dared to rebel against the powers that be would be killed—it was total chaos. The abuse and oppression were horrible, as these films so vividly depicted.

If you place yourself into the shoes of the main characters for a moment, both played by Mel Gibson in these two films, how would you have reacted? Would you have remained passive and allowed your world fall apart around you? Or, would you do as his characters did and fight back in the only way you could against the lawlessness? This may give you a better sense of who the Ku Klux Klan was and why they evolved into the organization they did during the Reconstruction. In *Braveheart*, it was William Wallace and his band of warrior-poets trying

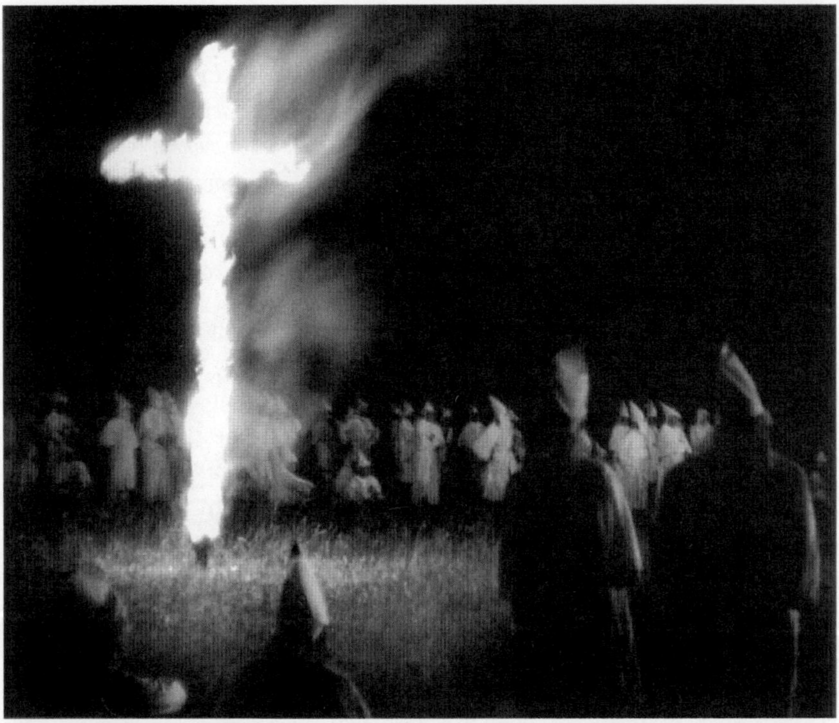

Members of the DeLand-area KKK burning a cross at one of their meetings. *Courtesy of the State of Florida Archives—Florida Memory Project.*

to gain freedom from tyranny; in *The Patriot*, it was the militia made up of angry farmers trying to salvage their lives; and in the South, it was the Ku Klux Klan trying to restore order and justice in a world that had neither. Each of these three groups was fighting for liberty against an overpowering and tyrannical force and in each case they succeeded.

There needs to be stated a strong emphasis on the differences between the first Klan from the 1860s to the 1880s; the second Klan from the 1900s to 1945; and finally the third Klan from 1945 to the present. The agendas of modern Klan groups are radically different, the urgency and necessity are absent and the justifications for their actions are weak. There is no defense for the modern Klan and its agenda at all, but much of what was happening during Reconstruction may justify this militia style in this group and its activities during that time period. Obviously not every action can be deemed acceptable, but the overall purpose and results of the actions can be seen as necessities—as it was in both of the aforementioned films.

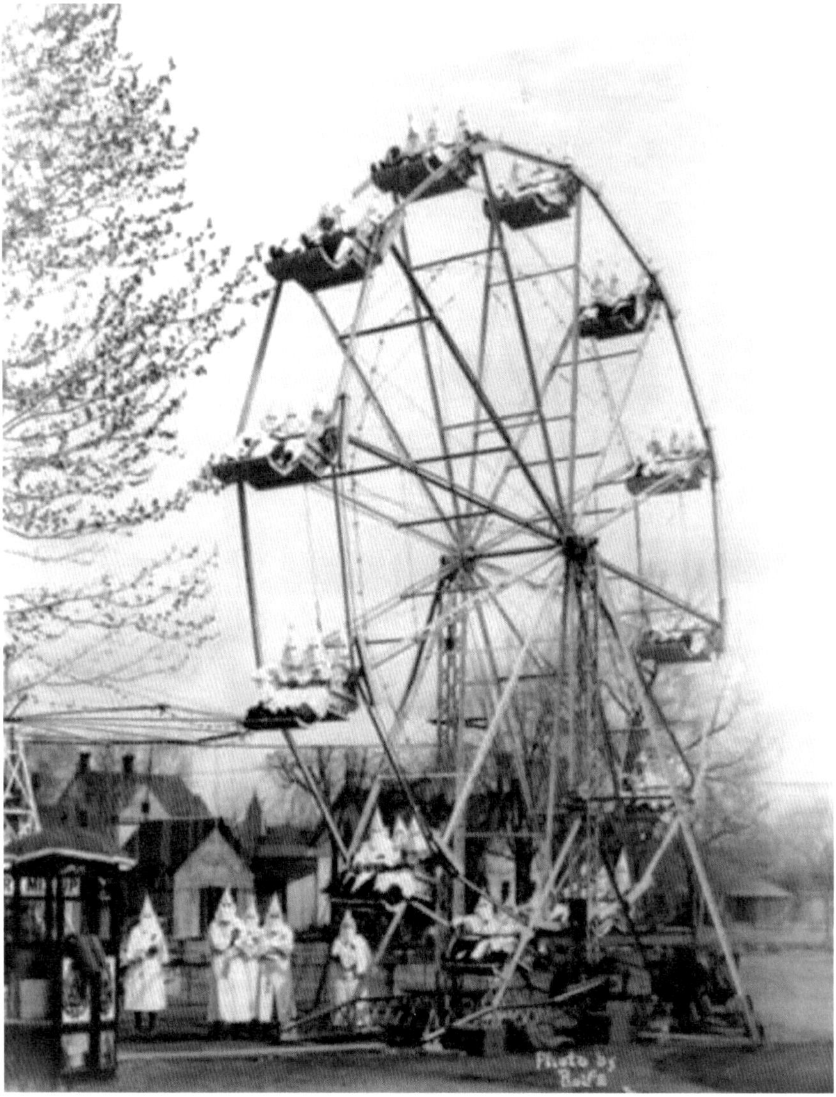

Klansmen proudly ride the Ferris wheel at the county fair. *Courtesy of the Library of Congress Archives.*

Into this new world was born Roy Cook in 1867. His father had been a member of the first Klan and as a young man Roy wanted to fight for the same rights and freedoms as his predecessors had. The problem was that the first Klan had all but completed their jobs during Reconstruction; the second Klan was quickly forming with their own ideas, ideals and agendas. The second Ku Klux Klan was officially founded in 1915 by William J. Simmons, an ex-minister and promoter of fraternal orders. The new Klan had a much larger agenda than its forerunner, for it added to "white supremacy" an intense nativism and anti-Catholicism; it was also anti-Semitic and opposed the cultural modernization of the Jazz Age and violations of alcohol, smoking and gambling laws. Directing their hate tactics toward Catholics, Jews and foreign-born, the Klan used tar and feathering, branding, mutilating and lynching to instill fear in their victims.

The Klan used others tactics to instill fear as well. The most significant, which later became a trademark of the Klan, was the burning of the cross. The fiery cross is said to be a "symbol representing the ideals of Christian civilization." The cross itself is a symbol of sacrifice and service to Christ. The fire signifies that "Christ is the light of the world." The light is said to "drive away the darkness and the gloom so a knowledge of truth dispels ignorance and superstition." Burning crosses were left as a mark to warn off those who had been violated in some other way by the Klan.

Consequently, the KKK's appeal was not sectional, and was aided after 1920 by the help of professional promoters Elizabeth Tyler and Edward Clarke. It spread rapidly throughout the North as well as the South. It furnished an outlet for the militant patriotism aroused by World War I and it stressed fundamentalism in religion. At its peak in the mid-1920s, its membership was estimated at four to five million strong, though some estimates are much lower, at only two million members.

Young Roy embraced the newly formed regime and dutifully attended weekly meetings, paid his dues even through the tough times of the Depression era and wore his KKK uniform with pride. He read all of the materials that were available on how to be a better Klansman, a better person within the regime and how to move America forward by bringing the new world order into politics, homes and churches across the nation. For Roy, this process started in his hometown of DeLand. Roy Cook was so proud of his newly found obsession and camaraderie with friends of similar interests that he attended other functions with them as well, including visiting the Volusia County Fair dressed in their best costumes for all to see.

While times had changed and so had the goals of the Klan, Roy found himself to be in the thick of it all when requested to give "special treatment" to members of the community that were a threat to the ways of the Klan and the Klan's way of forwarding their beliefs. Any member of the community that got in the way, got out of line or was

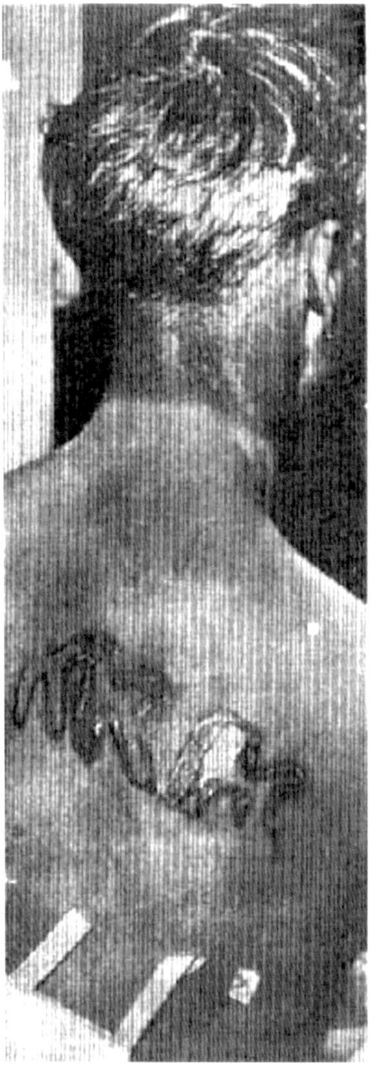

A man's back had been branded by local members of the KKK because he was considered to be an undesirable. *Courtesy of the State of Florida Archives—Florida Memory Project.*

in any way seen as an undesirable would immediately be dealt with harshly. While cross burning was the most common symbol or sign that the Klan had paid someone a visit, other methods of brutality were often implemented. It was not uncommon for people to show up at the local doctor's office the morning after the Klan had visited, showing a fresh brand across their back, biceps, thighs or chest; showing burn marks from having been tarred and feathered; having been whipped; or even women having been raped.

Roy had no problem with treating people this way; after all, he was doing his job and it was for a valiant cause, like his father and grandfather before him had done. The older he got the easier these "special treatments" became to administer. He took more and more pride and even pleasure in physical torture and even delighted in the thoughts that possible survivors would be emotionally and psychologically scarred for life. He began to draw further into the Klan itself and took little interest in anything that did not deal with the Klan itself or its goals. He stopped showing affection to his wife and children except for his son, whom he was grooming to take his place within the leadership of the Klan.

When he reached his thirties, Roy achieved the highest rank within the Klan—he had become the Grand High Dragon of the entire west Volusia County area. His attitude continued to change and he began to believe himself to be a godlike creature who was doing the Lord's work here on

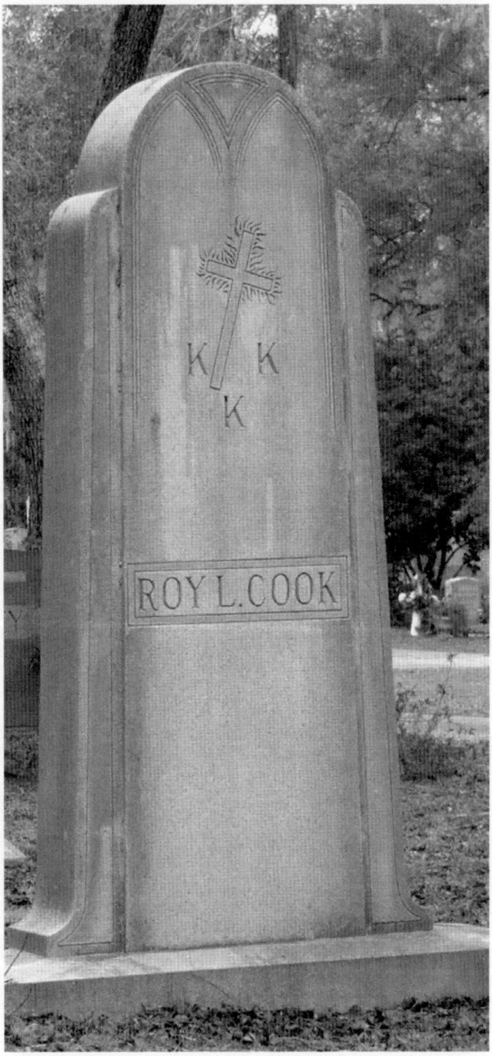

Roy Cook's headstone in Oakdale Cemetery in DeLand has been desecrated on many occasions by vandals. *Courtesy of the author.*

earth in order to rid society of the undesirables and to cleanse the earth of these "verminous" people. His son stood proudly at his side and now he too had a son, whom they both began to groom to ensure *his* place among the brotherhood. Even though times were changing, the KKK held fast to their beliefs and continued to move forward in their endeavors.

Roy Cook had become so fixated on his membership, duties and the KKK itself that it was all he lived for. Even though he was now getting older, he would warn people that even in the event of his death, he would remain in the area in spirit and continue to mete out the judgment of his beliefs in what the Klan was doing no matter what the cost or odds against him. He truly believed that even in death he would be able to rise from the grave and torture people as he saw fit. Little did he know how soon he would meet the grim reaper and be laid to rest, if truly laid to rest he was.

Roy passed away at only forty-four years of age. Some say he died because his heart gave out from having no love in it, that it simply hardened to the point that no blood could flow through it to his vital organs. Others claim that some of the locals that Roy once sought to exterminate gave him their own brand of vengeance and killed him while he slept one night. No matter what the cause of his death, he did die and was buried in Oakdale Cemetery in DeLand with a grand headstone befitting a true Grand High Dragon Klansman—it included a burning cross and the initials of his beloved KKK. It stands nearly ten feet tall and is oddly shaped to look almost human in the dark.

Many people claim that if you visit the cemetery at night, Roy Cook is keeping his promise. If you are of like mind with Roy Cook, the cross at the center of his headstone will burn brightly. If you stand near his grave on cold, misty nights in the fall, you can watch it transform into a man wearing a KKK robe. If you are one of the "verminous" people whom he sought to take out of this world, you will never be seen again.

Chapter 12

The Spirit Residents of the Cassadaga Hotel

When the Cassadaga Hotel opened in 1894 as a home away from home for visiting Spiritualists, psychics and mediums, no one knew at that time that the hotel would eventually become the home away from home for several restless spirits. It does make sense since mediums, psychics and Spiritualists live, work and visit the area, as well as tourists wanting to connect with passed on loved ones on the "other side." Some of these spirits find the Cassadaga Hotel to be a more welcoming place to reside than many other locations. Some believe that the Spiritualist camp of the town of Cassadaga also sits directly over a vortex of energy that attracts and sometimes holds spirits to this plane. Until science can come up with a way to prove that theory, we will just have to go by the fact that the Cassadaga Hotel and the surrounding Spiritualist camp have plenty of otherworldly residents.

While the hotel is in need of some renovations, it is not a four-star hotel and people who visit need to understand this fact. This is a place for people who want to get in touch with their spiritual self, get in touch with their loved ones, who may or may not have crossed over, and get away from it all. When I say "get away from it all," I do mean *all*. Each small room in the hotel gives visitors a good glimpse into the past; the old antique furniture, the small beds and the lack of televisions, radios or telephones brings you from the present into the past very quickly. There is no Internet service and cell phone service is intermittent at best. The bathrooms were added after a fire nearly consumed the entire hotel. Prior to indoor plumbing, there were shared lavatories and an outdoor community shower that the guests would use. Many of the newly added bathroom facilities are *very* small. With barely enough room to fit your knees between the toilet and wall, anyone over six feet, two inches tall is hereby forewarned! Most of the rooms have only a shower. The few that have tubs are a bit pricier, but if you enjoy a long hot bath as opposed to a standing shower, it's well worth the extra money to leisurely spend time in the old cast-iron claw foot tubs. There are no sinks in these small bathrooms in most of the rooms either. The sink is located in the main hotel room with a small medicine cabinet above it.

Almost every room in the Cassadaga Hotel boasts of having spirit activity of one form or another. There are the spirits of Alice Myers, her brother Arthur, Gentleman Jack, young sisters Sarah and Katlin, a cat that was a longtime resident of the hotel and reports of several other unknown and unnamed spirits. Some of these spirits have existed in the hotel for so long that many of the employees of the Cassadaga Hotel know their daily or nightly routines and can almost set their watches by their spirited activity.

While many visitors to the Cassadaga Hotel come to find their own family spirits, a few guests do come to find the resident spirits of the hotel. The staff is generally open about the ghosts and doesn't mind sharing personal experiences if time permits. One such worker was a dishwasher at the hotel

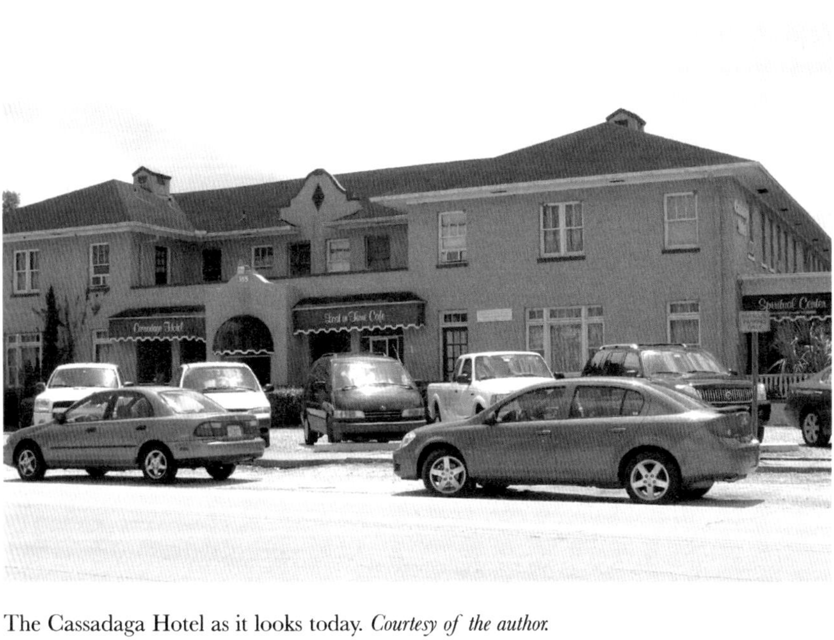

The Cassadaga Hotel as it looks today. *Courtesy of the author.*

several years ago. Prior to her employment there, a brother and sister were employed at the hotel—Alice was a maid and her brother Arthur was a maintenance man. They were both hard workers and enjoyed their jobs; the added benefit of part of their salary was that they got room and board. They each had a small room on the second floor of the hotel in the "staff" wing that they shared with many longtime resident mediums. During this time, it was rare to have overnight or weekend guests renting rooms on the second floor. Alice and Arthur would go about their daily work assignments and finish the end of the day with a good, hot meal in the dinning room. Arthur would cap off his night by having a couple of shots of gin, which he kept well hidden in his room. He would then descend the stairway into the lobby of the hotel and begin to play the piano for his sister, other workers and hotel guests. It was a nightly routine that nearly made Arthur a famous fixture at the hotel and everyone enjoyed his musical talents.

No one seems to remember when or how Alice passed away, but they do know that she died before her brother Arthur. Since Spiritualists believe that death is not an end but only a transition to another sphere of consciousness, I assume these kinds of details don't warrant remembering. But whenever and however Alice passed away, she did die while still working and residing at the Cassadaga Hotel. Alice used to live in room 19 and several guests reported, while unpacking their belongings in that room, that a woman's voice would say, "My name is Alice and I belong here." Some guests would become so unnerved that they wouldn't finish unpacking; they would put their belongings back into their suitcases and race down the steps and out the front door, never to return to the Cassadaga Hotel. It is said by many of the mediums at the hotel that Alice's spirit has since moved on and is now at rest while some guests of the hotel claim different. The guests say that Alice is still residing in room 19 and lets hotel guests know that she is present every chance she gets.

Arthur died shortly after his sister Alice, some say of a broken heart. But while there are disagreements over the fact of whether Alice's spirit is still present or not, there is no arguing that Arthur is still residing, working and playing the piano at the Cassadaga Hotel. Every evening, just as the kitchen staff is finishing up their final duties of the night, footsteps can be heard coming down the main staircase of the hotel. Several years ago, the dishwasher would hear the footsteps coming down the staircase and meet the spirit of Arthur, who was kind enough to bring her a shot of gin each night. She would always remind Arthur to be careful on the stairs and not to fall—apparently this may be how Arthur died. It is said by some that

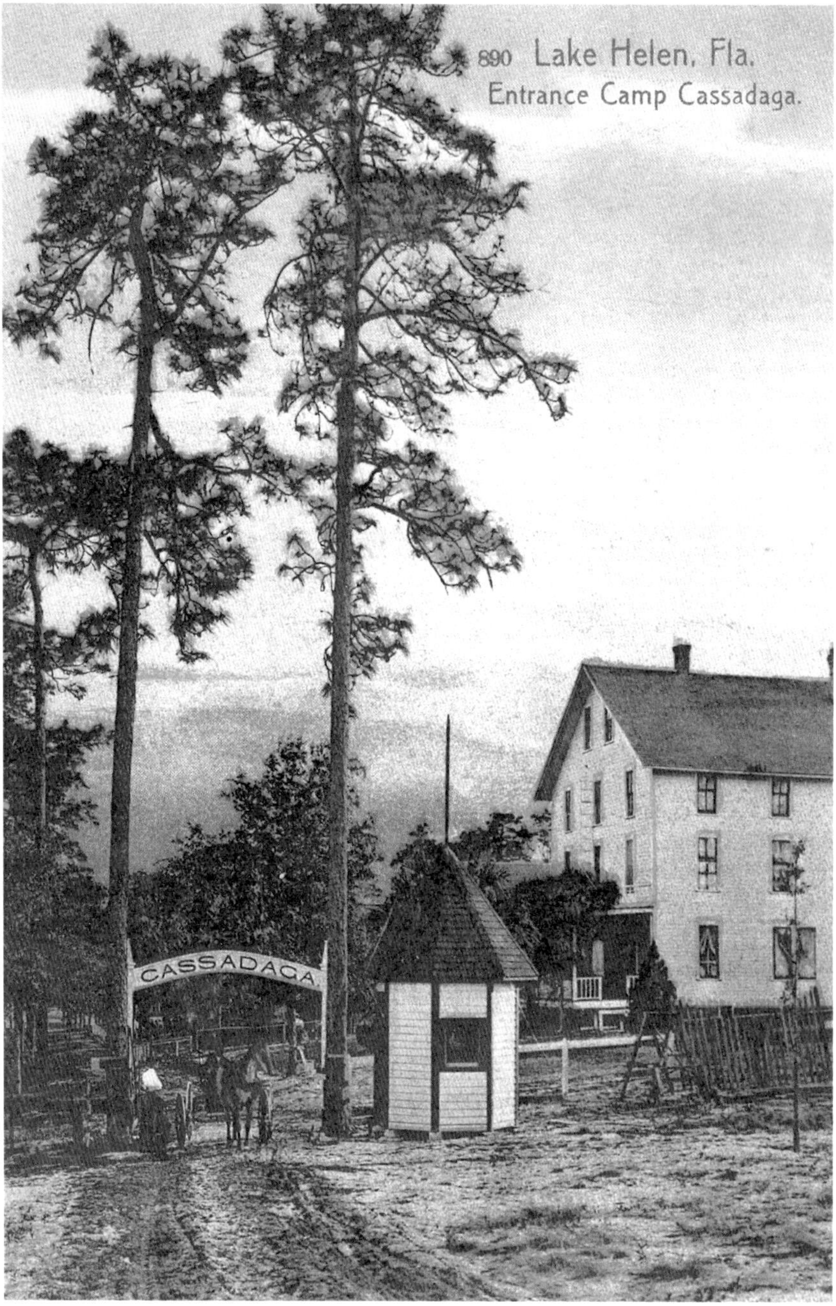

The entrance gate to Cassadaga in its heyday. *Courtesy of the State of Florida Archives—Florida Memory Project.*

he had gotten so drunk one night after his sister's death that he "tied one on" in his room, and when he descended the stairs to get more liquor, he lost his footing and broke his neck, and as a result died in the fall.

On many nights, Arthur can be seen standing at the foot of the stairs with a shot glass of gin in his hand. Shortly after that, the piano that still sits in the lobby of the Cassadaga Hotel begins to play all by itself. Or is it Arthur, still entertaining the employees, guests and other spirits of the Cassadaga Hotel?

The spirit of a ghost that everyone calls "Gentleman Jack" also still resides at the Cassadaga Hotel. Gentleman Jack's origins are also a bit cloudy. Some claim that he was a traveling salesman that frequented the hotel on his trips from the north through central Florida. One thing that we do know is that Gentleman Jack is one of the most active spirits at the Cassadaga Hotel and he is definitely a ladies' man! Gentleman Jack always rented the same room on the first floor in the hotel when he was taking a break from his travels—now room 10. During Jack's time, the hotel wasn't as long as it is now. The hotel fire destroyed most of the original hotel, and when they rebuilt it, they lengthened the building itself by nearly double. It seems the demand for rooms in the Spiritualist camp were on the rise. When visitors rent Jack's room and encounter his spirit, he only moves about half-way through room 10. Some believe that this is because the rest of room 10 never existed in Jack's time.

Gentleman Jack is a true ladies' man. Whenever women stay in the room or even enter the room, Jack makes his presence known. He will make a cold chill go through the room and you can smell bay run aftershave and even cigar smoke; however, when women are not present, Gentleman Jack is nowhere to be found. Gentleman Jack is in no way threatening, even with men. He does, however, prefer the company of ladies and he sometimes physically interacts with women by touching their hair, tugging on their clothing or even by lightly touching their arm or shoulders.

Gentleman Jack likes to hang out in the bathroom area of what is now room 10, one of the largest rooms in the hotel, complete with a full-sized bathroom and living room area. The bathroom in room 10 used to be a bedroom before the fire. Since most of the bedroom area and all of the living room area were not in the original hotel, Gentleman Jack never passes that imaginary half-way point. Gentleman Jack has been documented in this room by paranormal investigators and ghost hunters on many occasions, as well as by overnight visitors to the hotel. Although no one, including these investigators, is sure of why Gentleman Jack is stuck or chooses to remain behind at the Cassadaga Hotel, everyone who has experienced his presence knows that he will remain an otherworldly resident for a very long time—as long as the ladies will keep him company from time to time.

Sarah and Katlin are two sister spirits that still reside at the Cassadaga Hotel. These active, spirited little girls still roam the halls of the second floor, playing, running, singing and laughing their way through the afterlife. The girls are quite friendly with hotel guests and are always in a playful mood. Many guests of the hotel have seen the girls dancing and running down the halls on the second floor. They have been heard laughing and singing and on the rare occasion that another child is present in the hotel, they like to play with that child's toys.

One of the hotel rules is that no children under the age of eighteen are allowed to stay at the hotel unless accompanied by an adult. Even with an accompanying adult, having children around is frowned upon. Remember, this is a place for getting in touch with your spiritual side or for contacting the dead. Young children may not understand these concepts unless raised around them, and the thought of actually speaking with the dead may give some children nightmares or worse—therapy could be in their near future if they have a bad experience. With that stated, it is unclear why Sarah and Katlin were once residents of the hotel. It may be that their parents were part of the staff that lived on the second floor, or they could have been a part of a Spiritualist family that lived at or visited the camp early on. What is known is that the girls seem to have no idea that they are no longer among the living and they continue about their daily games, dances and songs in their afterlife at the Cassadaga Hotel.

Room 3 is host to another interesting and longtime resident spirit at the Cassadaga Hotel. Many years ago, a stray cat showed up and took up residence at the hotel. No one seemed to mind and the cat quickly became a fixture of the hotel. He would wander through the hotel, meeting and greeting all guests in order to get a good petting and possibly a free bite to eat. He would lazily sleep in the sun on the veranda when he wanted warmth, and when the weather turned sour, he would find a cozy place to rest in the hotel's lobby.

There have been many reports from various guests over the years of seeing and experiencing this phantom feline in several locations throughout the hotel. Many people see him still lying on the ledge of the veranda in the bright morning sunlight when they are exiting their hotel room on the veranda side. Once they turn to lock their door and turn back to see the sweet kitty blissfully resting on the ledge, he is no

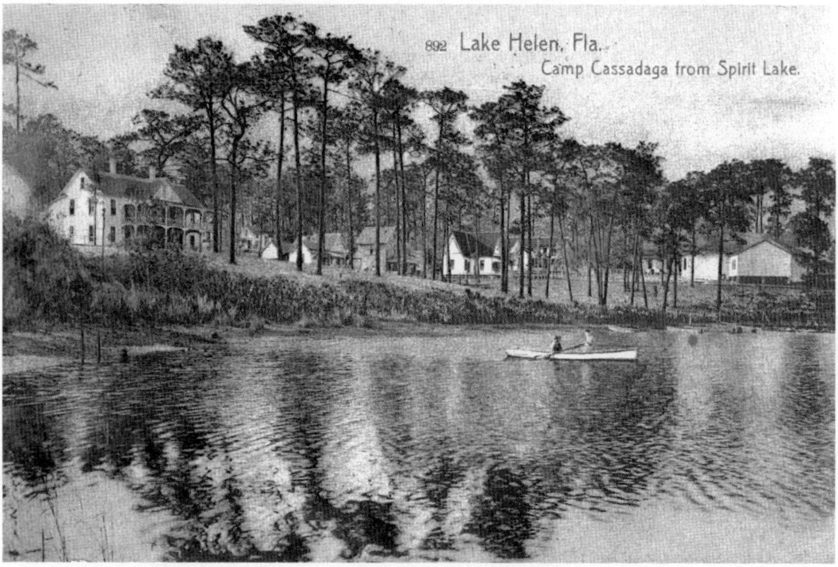

View of the Cassadaga Hotel taken from Spirit Pond. *Courtesy of the State of Florida Archives—Florida Memory Project.*

longer there. When they inquire at the desk or of one of the employees as to where the cat has gotten off to, they are always told that the cat is no longer among the living. Similar sightings occur in the dining area, lobby, second-floor hallway and front porch of the hotel, all with the same results—the kitty is not really there, he's only there in spirit.

There have also been reports of couples sleeping in room 3 that are awoken in the middle of the night to the feeling of a cat jumping up onto the bed. He will walk across the mattress and curl up between the two people, snuggling into the small of their backs. When one or the other person wakes up to see what just happened, there is no cat or anything else in the bed. In the morning, when they ask the staff about a cat being in room 3, they are told that the spirit cat frequents that room and likes to cuddle up with the living while they sleep.

No matter what the reason that you visit the beautiful Spiritualist camp of Cassadaga, whether it be to get in touch with your spiritual side, find or speak to a long-ago passed-away loved one or just to get away from it all and relax in the peaceful atmosphere, one thing is certain—you won't be disappointed by the ghosts who greet you, entertain you and make you smile at the Cassadaga Hotel.

Chapter 13
The Ghost Town of St. Francis

There are many ghost towns—or should I say, towns filled with ghosts—in Florida, but when someone says "ghost town," most people think of silver or gold mines in towns in the West that turned to dust once the mines stopped producing. Florida has its own version of gold. It is known by many names: Florida gold, liquid sunshine or, put simply, orange juice. This healthy, sweet, natural source of vitamins and energy became a staple crop and a booming financial industry early in Florida's history. One man responsible for a special touch when growing oranges was named Lue Gim Gong. Mr. Gong came to DeLand in 1888. He perfected a citrus tree on which the fruit would ripen in September but could remain on the tree for up to four years and still be good! This orange won Mr. Gong the Silver Wilder Medal from the Department of Agriculture in 1911, the only time it was ever awarded for citrus. Mr. Gong—or, as he was better known, the "Citrus Wizard"—died in 1925 and was laid to rest in Oakdale Cemetery in DeLand.

With this ingenious new way to produce oranges, many towns cropped up with citrus groves all over the state. There were three prosperous towns only four miles outside of DeLand in the late 1800s: Crow's Bluff, Hawkinsville and one known as St. Francis. Over one hundred years ago, these three towns were conveniently located on the banks of the St. John's River so trade could be more easily accomplished via the steamboats on the river, and St. Francis quickly became a thriving trade town.

The town of St. Francis rose in industry and commerce faster than even DeLand did at the time. At the turn of the century, St. Francis had its own hotel, a general store, livery stable, its very own post office, several

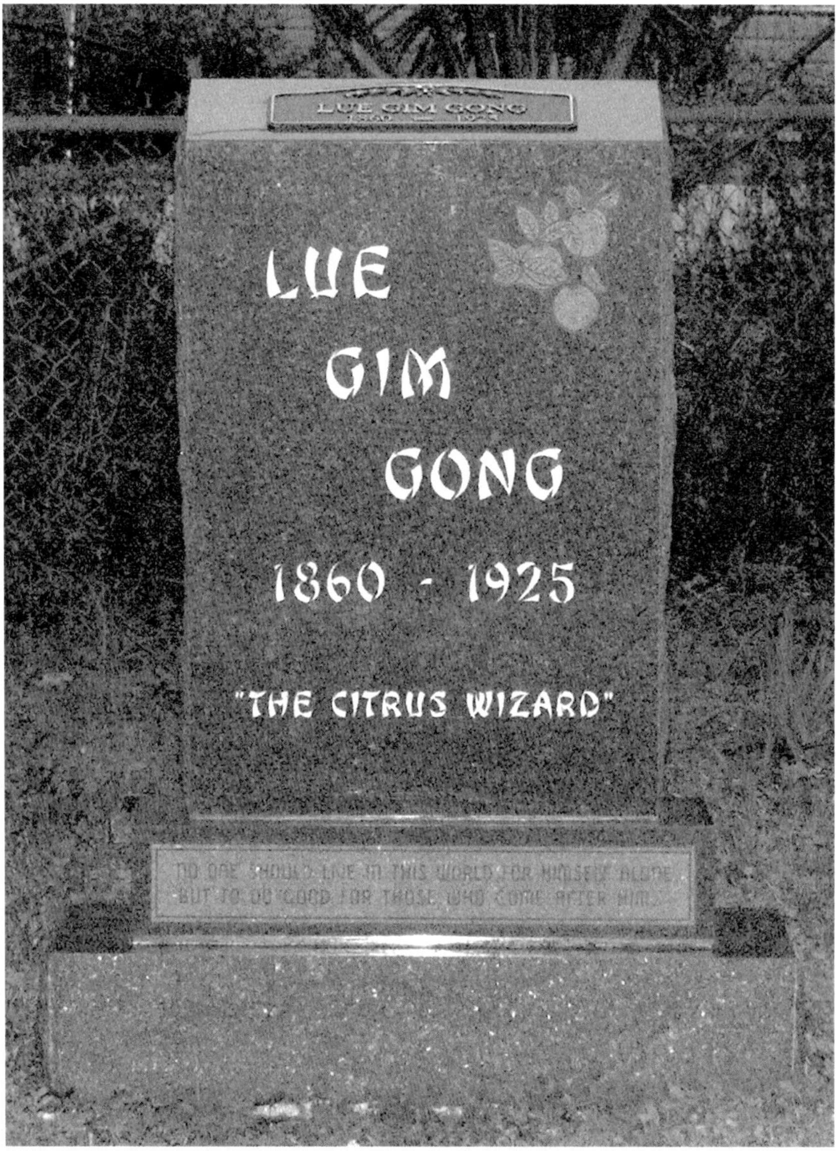

Lue Gim Gong's headstone seen today in Oakdale Cemetery. His epitaph reads: "No one should live in this world for himself alone but to do good for those who come after him." *Courtesy of the author.*

cottages and plenty of two-story cypress homes to accommodate its growing population. Steamboats would unload goods and supplies there on trips down the river from Palatka, as well as goods being brought in by ox-drawn wagons. These goods included lumber, citrus and other staples that would allow the townspeople to begin a prosperous life in St. Francis.

People grew vegetables and fruits in large fields. Long, specially designed furrows were set aside for watermelon and levees were created for cultivating rice. Citrus groves of all types were planted and thrived, but oranges were the main citrus fruits produced in St. Francis. During the winters of 1894 and 1895, there were several freezes that damaged the citrus crops, which never fully recovered. With the main source of income now gone from the town, the people started to move on as well. Fires destroyed some of the wooden buildings, and a hurricane in the 1920s all but finished off the once-thriving town. The final blow would be the railroad's arrival in central Florida, thanks to Henry Flagler.

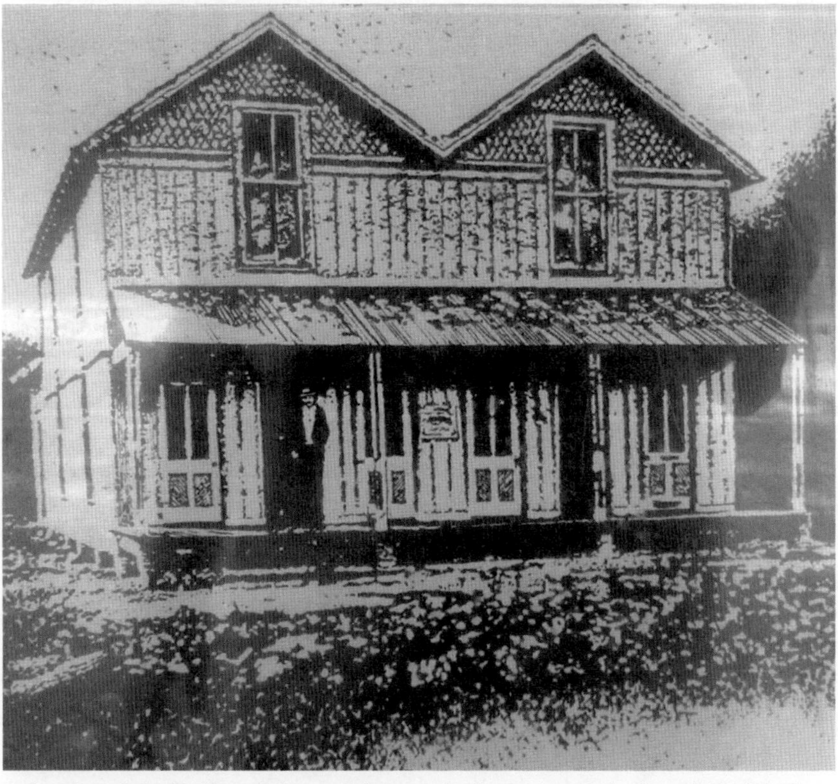

A drawing of the St. Francis General Store at the beginning of the Francis Trail in the Ocala National Forrest. *Courtesy of the author.*

The railroad was a blessing for many areas—it meant that more products, goods and even workers could find their ways to remote areas of the state—but it put other areas along the rivers in danger. St. Francis was doomed by this technological modernization. By 1935, the town was just a memory and all that remained of the once-beautiful buildings, including a couple of homes in the Victorian style, quickly vanished. The true story of how life was and how people lived in St. Francis is unclear. Vandals and looters have taken or destroyed all that remains of this beautiful but secluded trade town. Now all that remains is the partial foundation of one of the homes or possibly a business building of some sort—we will never know for sure.

The town of St. Francis is now a highlighted trail hike along Florida's Trail Associations routes through the West Volusia area. It is now illegal to dig, collect or even use a metal detector in what used to be the town of St. Francis. The Francis Trail, a hike 7.7 miles long, crosses the old fields that were once used to raise vegetables. The furrows and ridges can still be seen in the ground and are remnants of the early watermelon plantings. There are also pilings from the old dock that are still visible, as well as many large cypress stumps and the "tramway"—a narrow-gauge rail bed—that are left behind from the defunct logging industry, all on the outskirts of what used to be St. Francis.

While all but one physical attribute of St. Francis remains in what is now the Ocala National Forest, the spirits of the people who once lived there still go about their daily business. There have been many reports from people hiking the Francis Trail of seeing people off in the distance seemingly working in a field. When the hikers walk off the trail to see what all the fuss is about, momentarily losing sight of the workers in the dense brush, no one is there.

Since this section of the woods is very dense and filled with wildlife, it is a favorite for local hunters. It is also a year-round recreational place for people who own four-wheel-drive trucks, dirt bikes and ATVs, and fishermen and other outdoor enthusiasts enjoy it as well. When people are attending to their personal brand of outdoor recreation, they report sounds of trees being cut with a saw, which is illegal to do in Ocala National Forest. The few who have been brave enough to venture into the thick brush to find the culprits can still hear the sounds, but never get close enough to find them. It's as if the sounds move farther away the closer the investigators get. Sounds of squeaking gates, whistling and harmonica and banjo music have also been heard in the area that was once the town of St. Francis.

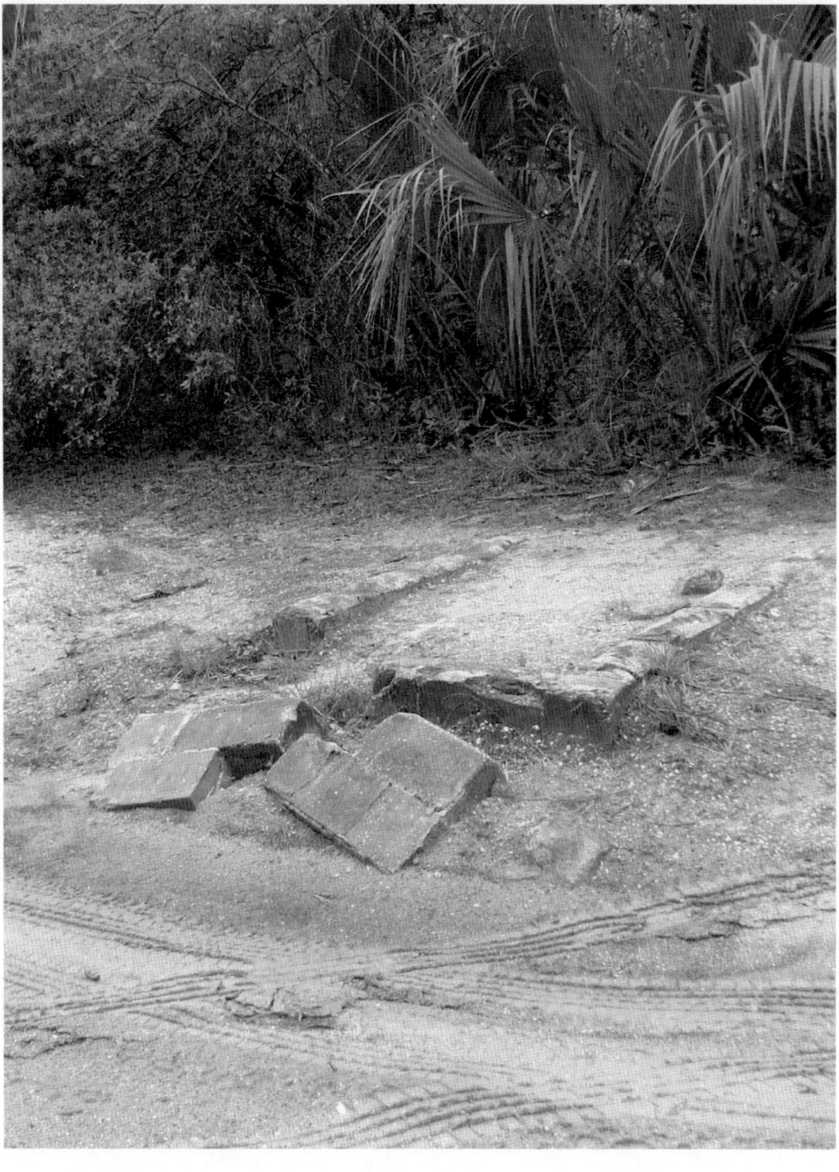

The only remaining evidence that the town of St. Francis once existed in what is now the Ocala National Forest. *Courtesy of the author.*

Two decades after the demise of the town, an explorer venturing through Florida camped out one night on the banks of the St. John's River, where the steamboats would stop to unload supplies for the townsfolk of St. Francis. The gentleman made a small fire to cook his freshly caught fish dinner and to keep warm in the overnight hours, but he didn't get much sleep that night. He told tales of hearing voices coming from the old town, continually having the feeling of being watched all night and he felt a "presence" all around him for the entire night.

We can only assume that since people lived and died in St. Francis for many decades that their spirits have remained behind to keep trading goods, growing oranges, raising watermelons and just enjoying life in the afterlife in their very own ghost town.

Chapter 14

The Devil's Chair

In 1848, in the town of Hydesville in western New York, two young sisters named Maggie and Katie Fox supposedly began communicating with the ghost of a murdered peddler. The sisters, in a sort of crude séance, would ask questions of the spirit, and the spirit would answer back with mysterious knocks or raps. Many people, including their mother, were amazed at what seemed to be genuine contact with the dead. The Fox sisters gave public performances of their newly found gifts as mediums and quickly rose to fame in the annals of U.S. history.

Both sisters eventually admitted that they had actually faked the sounds. There had been no murdered peddler. It had all been a prank. The young women even demonstrated how they had done it. Their fame drove them both to drinking, and they both died penniless after suffering tragedies. By then, the belief had taken on a life of its own, as well as helping to form a religion called Spiritualism; which is still practiced today.

Spiritualists follow the teachings of the Bible and believe in the Christian God, but only as "Infinite Intelligence." There are no stipulations of what "Infinite Intelligence" is, except that it can be reached directly through its followers for personal and spiritual experiences of growth. Spiritualists do not believe in right or wrong, but rather in spiritual progression.

Once the Spiritualist movement had begun a camp, its followers formed in Lily Dale, New York. Situated on Lake Cassadaga, the members of the camp practiced their religion in peace. One of the members of the Lily Dale Spiritualist Camp was young George Colby. During a séance when he was young, he had a vision of starting his own camp in the South someday. His vision would become a reality in 1875, when Colby was led by his spirit guide, "Seneca," through a hilly area in central Florida. Amazingly enough, Cassadaga means "rock beneath the water" in the Native American Seneca tribe's native tongue.

When Colby arrived in Florida, he was suffering from tuberculosis. He claims to have been healed by drinking water from a freshwater spring that is still located on what was at one time his homestead. After purchasing thirty-five acres of land and starting the Cassadaga Spiritualist Camp, he deeded the land over to the newly formed and incorporated Cassadaga Spiritualist Camp Meeting Association in 1895; it has been a spiritual place for psychics, mediums and healers to live, learn, love and grow ever since.

While Cassadaga remains a small town, with only fifty-seven acres of land and a population of only four hundred, it is one tourist spot that many people find when visiting the central Florida area. Situated between DeLand and Lake Helen, Cassadaga is the sleepiest little town in the area. Currently, there are fifty-five homes with twenty-five mediums living in Cassadaga, but none of the people own the land. They own their homes, but the land belongs to the camp. There is a small post office, a privately owned hotel, the camp's bookstore, a temple building, a small lake and a New Age store within the city limits; you won't find a McDonald's, Starbucks coffee, ATMs or even a school in town.

On the border of Cassadaga and Lake Helen is the Lake Helen/Cassadaga Cemetery. Folks in Cassadaga will tell you that they don't have a cemetery, and technically this is true since they share their cemetery with the city of Lake Helen. They will also be quick to tell you that the legend of the Devil's Chair is just a rumor. No one is quite sure how the story began—maybe it was the neighbors from Lake Helen, who often raised more than an eyebrow at their new Spiritualist neighbors; maybe it was tourists, who thought that Spiritualism had something to do with devil worship or witchcraft, neither of which is the case; or maybe it was just a good old-fashioned storytelling hour late one dark night in the cemetery that caught on and has been retold ever since. No matter how the story began, there are many people who believe the tale is true and even those who claim to have been visited in the chair by the dark lord himself. Since the stories began to circulate long after the camp's opening, we can be pretty sure that it had nothing to do with any of the residents of the camp.

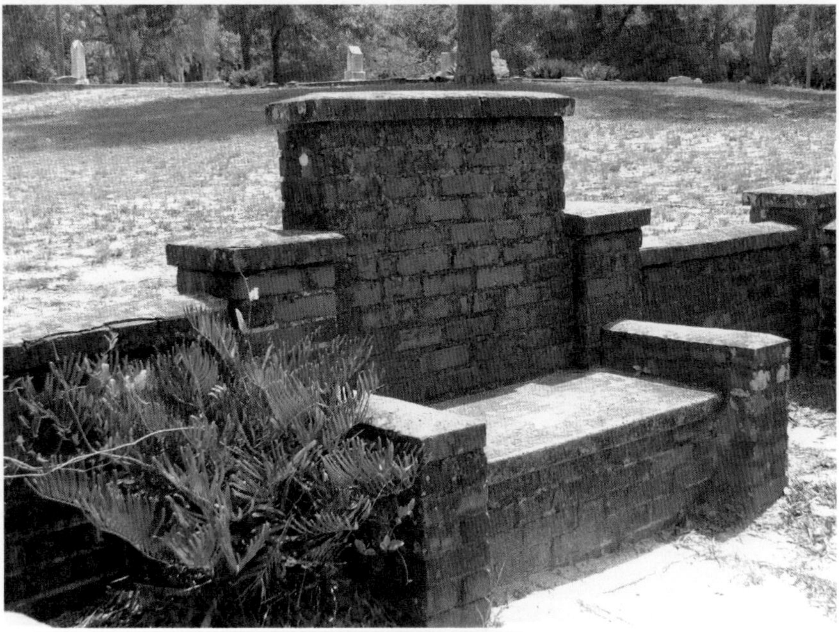

The legendary Devil's Chair in the Lake Helen Cemetery. *Courtesy of the author.*

There are a few privately owned sculptures, also known as headstones, in the Lake Helen/Cassadaga Cemetery that are in the shape of a large chair or bench. They are made from red brick and some are painted white. The original chair, which is said to be the true devil's chair, was designed by a brokenhearted man who lost his soul mate. He had the chair made so he could spend longer periods of time visiting with her during a time when mourning benches were not common and very expensive. Since there are four of these types of chairs in the cemetery, no one knows for sure which one is the devil's chair.

The story goes something like this. If you find the devil's chair and sit in it at midnight, the devil himself will join you and speak with you about your wishes. If you offer him a bottle of cold beer, he will grant you a wish by the time he has finished the bottle. If you sit on his chair at midnight on All Hallows' Eve, he will hold you there until he feels like letting you go.

Because of the stories and purported sightings of ghosts and dark apparitions over the years, the cemetery has been the victim of a great deal of vandalism and damage. Many local youths come out late at night and taunt one another into sitting in each of the four chairs. One young lady not only claims to have seen a ghost in the cemetery one night, but when she sat in the chair at midnight on Halloween the devil held her in place for several minutes. She was frightened almost to death and ran from the cemetery, never to enter it again.

The brave few who actually offer Satan that cold bottle of beer never stay long enough to find out if the dark lord has actually drank the libations. However, when they return in the morning, the bottle is always empty! Could the story be true? Or is it more likely that the local Lake Helen police officers had a nightcap before heading home after their shift late at night?

Chapter 15

The Horrors at the Honey Processing Plant

When Ponce de León landed in what is now Florida, looking for the fountain of youth, he may have actually found it in what many Native Americans already knew—the saw palmetto and its flowers that, once pollinated by bees, can produce quality honey. The fruit from the saw palmetto was also found to have healthy benefits, especially for older men. Saw palmetto fruit or berries were used by elderly Native American men to decrease the swelling of the prostate, to enhance their libido and inhibit hair loss; the tasty berries also helped to correct many urinary tract complications. The Spanish began exporting the berries in the early 1600s to show this miracle cure and age rejuvenator that had been discovered in the New World and was named "the spring of life" by the Native Americans.

Although small concentrations of saw palmettos can be found from southern Mississippi to South Carolina, Florida is recognized with the only density of saw palmettos large enough to gather the berries and honey in commercial quantities. The area running from approximately Sarasota to Miami has in recent years been identified as the "palmetto belt," as it is only in this region that saw palmettos bear fruit consistently and in quantities that support the high demand for commercial honey and berry production. High humidity and steady heat, with the absence of winter's low temperatures, make Florida the perfect location for the saw palmetto.

The saw palmetto grows very slowly, with trunks that lay flat on the ground that eventually turn ninety degrees skyward to support a palm head that can be anywhere from four to six feet in diameter. Most palmetto patches grow four feet tall; however, some varieties of this palm can grow as high as twenty feet tall and live to be over seven hundred years old. The seeds from the saw palmetto can take up to six months to germinate and up to six years to bear fruit. The honey bee has become the primary pollinator of the saw palmetto, producing a secondary agricultural crop to this industry worth $120 million a year.

During the 1800s and early to mid-1900s, Florida's newest industries—other than citrus, lumber, cattle and cotton—were the collecting and processing of turpentine and honey. Turpentine production and demand fell off sharply after the end of the Civil War and even further after WWI had ended. Honey production, however, stayed in high demand, with many apiaries popping up across the Southern states. With the many citrus groves, saw palmettos and tupelo flowers growing in central Florida, an entrepreneur in DeLand decided he would cash in on this golden sweetener and health aid. He opened up a honey processing plant in an area that is now about a mile east of the US-92 and US-17/92 intersection in DeLand.

Since many men were still overseas serving in the military and child labor laws were not yet in place as they are today, children were often employed to work in various farming areas. It was inexpensive labor that could be had for pennies a day. Most young boys didn't mind the work and one benefit would be a mouthful of the sweet honey once or twice a day, plus they could always sneak a little home to their mothers in a carefully concealed jar for use in cooking when the boss wasn't looking. The hours were long, the days were hot and the work was dangerous, but none of the boys working at the honey processing plant seemed to mind—most days, it was more of a game than work to them.

The owner of the plant was a strict employer. If he caught the boys clowning around or shirking their duties, they would be whipped with his belt. While he was kind enough to provide them with simple meals

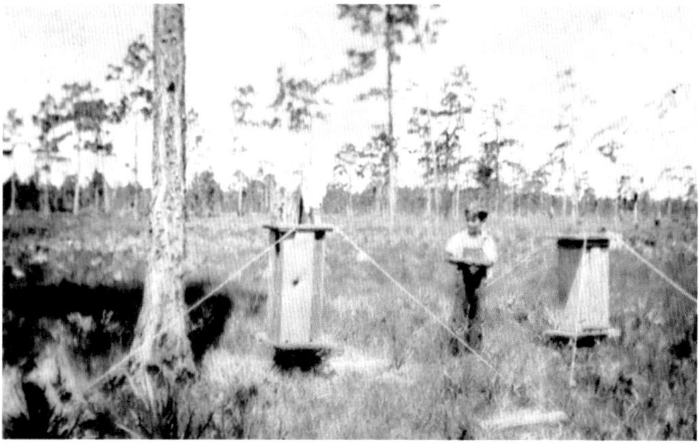

A child laborer and some of the beehives at the honey processing plant. *Courtesy of the State of Florida Archives—Florida Memory Project.*

of homemade bread, a cup of milk, an occasional slice of cheese or even an orange that he would steal from the groves next door, he never let his little employees forget who the boss *really* was. The boys kept their noses to the grindstone from dawn to dusk, six days a week, for most of the year. They did attend school part of the year, but they wondered who needed an education when you already had a job.

At the peak of production at the plant, five young boys were working together—David, Benjamin (or Benny, as he was called), Luke, Daniel and Robert. The boys got along well with one another on most days, but fought like brothers on other days. David, being the oldest, would sometimes help the younger boys to complete their work if he saw they were falling behind. If one fell behind, they would all fall behind and that meant a whipping for sure. Benny would always walk home with Robert and they would talk about going fishing on their days off from the plant. Luke and Daniel would walk together, too, as they were brothers, and David usually stayed at the plant, sleeping in the toolshed at the east end of the property. It seems that his father had gone off to fight in the war and as he had no mother or siblings to speak of, there was really no sense in walking all the way to the other end of town to sit alone in an empty house. The boss never caught on and David felt like he was the king of his own little castle. He also took it upon himself to be a sort of night watchman at the plant. If he heard bears, raccoons or thieves coming after the honey, he would make as much noise as he could in the shed by banging tools together and the culprit would quickly skedaddle! There had previously been problems with vagrants coming into the grounds at night to steal honey and David had caught them once before. His employer rewarded him by giving him a shiny new nickel as he hauled the culprits off to the police station.

One night, David wasn't feeling very well and when the other boys were leaving they saw him enter the toolshed. No one had known that David was living in the shed until that moment. Being fun-loving boys, they all decided to play a prank on David and sneak up on him to give him a fright. The plan backfired and David caught them as they approached the toolshed windows. He quickly bolted out of the door and grabbed poor Daniel by his arm and began screaming at him. The other boys tried to help and the next thing any of them knew was that a gun had been fired. Their employer had heard the commotion and thought it was thieves trying to steal tools out of the shed so he fired a warning shot to ward them off.

The boys stopped writhing around on the ground in the tangled wrestling match and looked up at their employer in shock. He made the

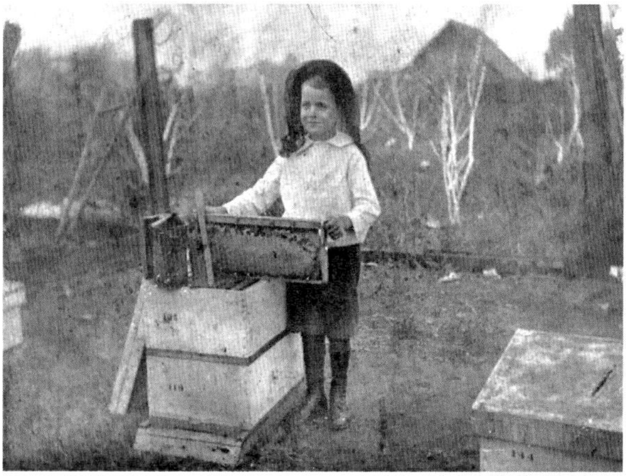

A young boy working as a beekeeper. *Courtesy of the State of Florida Archives—Florida Memory Project.*

boys line up against the north wall of the toolshed, where he immediately started whipping the boys with his belt. He was a strict man and they had startled him, but he had also been drinking a bit of moonshine that night during a poker game with some of his buddies. The beatings continued until Robert fell to the ground, crying. Daniel and Benny rushed over to him to see if they could help him and their employer knocked them both to the ground. He finally stopped and threw his belt on the ground and told the boys to leave; he would "finish dealing with them in the morning," he said. He wanted to get back to his poker game and his booze. He walked toward the office building and slammed the door hard.

The boss left the boys lying on the ground near the toolshed. A bond quickly formed, a bond akin to that experienced by men who go to war and face battles together. David picked Robert up and carried him into the shed. The other boys followed them in and noticed that David wasn't just spending the night there out of laziness—he had been living in the shed for quite a while. He had a small cot, an old chair, one set of dishes and silverware, a tin cup, a towel and a photo of his father hanging on the wall next to his bed. The other boys soon realized how lonely David must have been, living in a toolshed alone and with only them working beside him during daylight hours.

As David started to attend to Robert's wounds, the other boys helped bandage one another up and Benny began asking David personal questions that David wasn't ready to answer or deal with at first. When an hour or so had passed and all the boys had quieted down and were on the mend, David sat quietly on the edge of his bed and wept. He missed his mother, "Why did she have to die?" he asked. None of the other boys knew how to answer his question, nor did they know how to deal with his loss. David then began talking openly about his mother and father and how much he missed them both. He yearned for the day when his father would return home and the two could be together and have some semblance of a family life once again. The other boys had believed that David enjoyed his job at the honey plant but soon found out differently. He actually despised working there and wanted to go to school and be with his father. They tried to comfort him as best they could and David did start to feel better; it was the first time he had been able to talk with anyone about his loss and his feelings since his father had joined the service.

They all decided to spend the night in the toolshed with David. They knew Robert was injured and felt he shouldn't be moved, so they gave him the cot. David was obviously still distraught and shouldn't be left alone. It was Friday night and sometimes they would go fishing all night after work, so they wouldn't be missed at home. They talked about their families, their feelings and their futures and the night sped by into the early morning hours. They laughed and cried together and became close friends and sealed that friendship with an oath. The all clasped their hands together and recited: "The five of us will always be, friends until the end of eternity!" Little did they know how soon the end of eternity would be for their young lives.

While the boys were bonding and healing from their wounds, their employer was still playing poker with his buddies and still drinking booze. The more money he lost, the more he drank and the more he drank, the angrier he'd get. By 1:00 a.m., he had lost over $500 and had drunk two bottles of moonshine. His thoughts kept going back to how the boys had "misbehaved" and how he had had to reprimand them. Every time he envisioned the belt lashing out onto one of their backsides, he would feel it again and again as if it were still happening. His anger grew until he started lashing out verbally at his poker pals. They, however, were not young boys who were afraid of him. Arguments ensued, accusations of cheating were bantered about, tempers flared and fisticuffs were just around the corner.

At 2:30 a.m., the boys had all fallen asleep in the toolshed. David would occasionally wake up and check on the younger boys, especially Robert, since he was injured more than the others. He could hear the men laughing and yelling, mostly yelling. He couldn't make out exactly what they were saying, but he knew with his employer's temper that he needed to keep the other boys quiet if they did wake up. If they were all found sleeping in the shed, not only would David lose his temporary home, but they would probably be beaten nearly to death. Since David now felt like an older brother who would be caring for and protecting his younger, adopted brothers, he couldn't let that happen ever again. The men who were still in the main office of the honey plant were now no longer playing cards—all they could do was drink and argue, and argue they did.

One of the men stood up to go outside and relieve himself of the recently ingested liquor when he noticed a shadow in the window of the toolshed. It was David. David hadn't seen the man standing outside. He was merely trying to check on Luke and Benny, who were sleeping on some boxes stacked by the window. The man hurried back into the office and informed his inebriated friend and fellow drunken poker player that he may have an intruder in the toolshed. At first, the employer didn't believe the other man and they began to argue about how drunk he was and that he must be seeing things. The two men got louder and louder and they started pushing one another around. It then came to blows.

David heard the argument and quickly locked the toolshed door. He covered Benny and Luke with some burlap sacks so even if someone looked in the window they couldn't be seen. Daniel, who rested on the floor next to Robert's cot, was situated in such a way as to not be seen from any of the windows. Now all David had to do was find a place to conceal himself and they would all be safe. As David reached up to grab a tarp to hide under, it caught on the edge of a metal rake and the rake and a few adjacent tools came crashing down around him.

The men in the office heard the commotion and headed out the door and toward the toolshed. The boy's drunken employer said, "I guess you were right, Bubba. Let's go catch us some thieves." One man had a handgun, another had a shotgun and another grabbed a kerosene lamp to light their way in the dark. When they arrived at the toolshed, the boy's employer tried to open the door but it had been locked by David. He assumed that it had been locked by the thief, now holed up in the shed. The men banged on the door, yelling and screaming. One of the men fired his shotgun into the air, which woke all the boys. David held his finger to his lips, motioning for them all to stay quiet. Daniel jumped into the cot with Robert and the boys held one another tightly. Luke and Benny followed suit.

The men were still outside making a rowdy, loud commotion. Even if the boys had been brave enough to yell out to the men and explain that it was only the boys in the shed, they would never have been heard. The ruckus continued for several minutes until finally the boys' employer yelled out, "I'm tired of dealin' with these boys. I need another drink." With that statement, the young boys breathed a sigh of relief. They heard the men's footsteps leading away from the toolshed and all thought that they were safe at last—they had no idea how wrong they were.

Just as the boys started to come out of their hiding places, they heard glass breaking outside the toolshed. They all quickly assumed their prior positions and kept as quiet as they could. They heard more glass break and now began to see light through the mesh of the burlap bags and holes in the tarps and blanket. At first, David thought it was sunrise coming through the windows, until he heard a maniacal voice shout out, "That's it boys! Burn it down! If the bastard won't come out on his own, we'll smoke him out or burn him out!" All of the men began laughing, yelling and shooting off their guns. Their drunken state had blurred their judgment and they now saw this as a game.

David feared for his life and for the lives of his brothers, so he started calling out as loud as he could that it wasn't a thief, that it was the boys, but he got no response. He tried to find the door in the darkened room and when he did he couldn't get the lock undone. Smoke began to billow into the toolshed from under the door, through the cracks in the wood floor and all around the window frames. All of the boys began yelling as loud as they could, but the men still didn't hear them. Benny even threw a box through the window to try to get their attention but this only confirmed to them that someone was in the shed who shouldn't be. David kept at the lock while the other boys did what they could to escape the inferno that was now consuming the small amount of oxygen left in the tiny space. The remaining windows broke with the heat of the fire, sending shattered glass throughout the small building and one shard hit Luke in the neck.

Benny tried to assist Luke, but as he made his way to him, he tripped over some of the tools that had fallen when David had reached up for the tarp earlier. When Benny fell, he hit his head on the corner of a box and knocked himself unconscious. Daniel was now trying to help David get the only door in the shed opened while Robert lay in the cot, still severely injured, unable to move and barely able to breath. None of the boys knew it at the time that their employer had finished beating him, but Robert had a broken collar bone, several broken ribs and a ruptured spleen.

Luke slumped over, his body falling next to Benny, where he finally bled to death. Benny simply never woke up and neither did Robert. Daniel collapsed from smoke inhalation and David eventually pried the hinges off the door. When the door fell in, there was a man standing just outside who fired one shot, killing the young boy instantly. The men, realizing what they had just done, knew they would hang for killing five young boys in such a heinous manner. They, too, made an oath that night—they would bury the boy's bodies under the beehives and never speak about this night again. If anyone asked or came looking for the boys, they would simply be told that the boys had left after work that night and that no one had seen them since. Many would assume that the boys had walked over to either Blue Springs or DeLeon Springs to go fishing or for a swim and drowned or might even have been attacked and killed by an alligator.

The men followed through with their plan. The following day, they put up another small toolshed where the old one had been. The boys were laid to rest in a common grave, keeping their oaths to one another. Beehives were set atop the unmarked burial site, and after a time, no one asked any more questions about the boys' whereabouts until the early 1980s.

After the honey plant failed because of the owner's severe drinking problem and guilt riddled memories of that fatal night, others tried and failed at businesses on the honey plant's old property. Finally, in 1984, a hotel was built on the very spot where the boys were buried. Almost immediately after opening, strange things began to be noticed by the hotel's staff and guests. There have been hundreds of reports over the years of hearing young boys playing in the corridors on the fourth floor. Laughter, giggling and even little running footsteps can all be heard on the fourth floor. There is also a room on the fourth floor that sits directly above where the old toolshed once stood. There is a spot in the corner of that room where temperature readings have been recorded at being over one thousand degrees Fahrenheit.

Many guests who rent that room vacate the premises in the middle of the night. They report children laughing, blankets being yanked off the bed, feeling hot when the air conditioning in the room is set to sixty-five degrees, having small objects moved or turn up missing and some have even seen five young boys standing at the foot of their bed, staring at them while they try to sleep. All of the boys appear to be badly burned and look red or orange in color. While guests don't always appreciate this kind of added bonus in a three-star hotel, some of the staff has come to expect the activity, while others refuse to even enter that room or venture onto the fourth floor.

The most frightening reports are those of guests and staff hearing young boys screaming from inside that room. When the front desk is called to assist whomever is in the room, the person reporting the incident is told that there is no one in that room. If the guest making the report becomes insistent and the staff does go up and check the room, they are always greeted by a hot wind that blows from inside the room through the door and the eerie sounds of young boys screaming in pain.

Chapter 16

The Poltergeist at the Putnam Hotel

When Henry DeLand moved to the area, he brought many of his friends and neighbors from northern New York with him. Several families came from DeLand's own hometown of Fairport while other homesteaders moved down from towns such as Buffalo, Brockport, Utica, Syracuse, Catskill, Benton Center and Troy. Alfred Putnam from Utica built and managed the Putnam Hotel. When the original hotel burned to the ground in 1917, Alfred had it rebuilt under the strict new laws that required all buildings in the area to be made of masonry products and it reopened its doors to the public and has stayed open ever since. When the Putnam Hotel reopened its doors in 1923, it was the first bona fide hotel in the DeLand area.

The Putnam Hotel was a beautiful place to stay in its heyday, with all of the upscale amenities that any affluent traveler could hope for. Beautiful marble floors gleamed in the sunlight that peeked through the massive window panes of the front windows of the hotel. Every room had its own bathroom facilities, complete with cast-iron claw foot tubs, and unlike the soon-to-be-opened DeLand Hotel, the rooms were spacious and grand. Every room had an Oriental rug placed perfectly in the center with just enough of the underlying hardwood floors showing to make a classy statement. The sunrooms to either side of the entryway of the hotel were perfect for sipping a cup of hot tea in the afternoon, reading a book or just visiting with other hotel guests. What is now a nightclub was once a grand English tavern that served the best brandy, champagne and cognac. Every evening a staff member would turn down your bed for you, and every morning they would tidy your room. There was a laundry service available as well as alterations and suit rentals in case you were attending a show at the Athens Theater. Many nights the management would make available entertainment provided to the hotel guests in the form of a violinist that would wander through the hotel's lobby, sunrooms and tavern until the wee hours of the morning. He would play classical music and it could be quite romantic for those in love. For a small "tip," he would play any song you requested. Life was grand at the Putnam Hotel.

Time, poor ownership and care have brought this formerly fine establishment to its knees. What was once DeLand's finest hotel establishment is now one of DeLand's dirty little secrets. The once-grand hotel is now run as a hotel and inexpensive apartments. Since the upkeep has been quite lacking over the past couple of decades, it no longer attracts the fine clientele it once did. The nightclub in the lower section of the hotel is open year-round, and at one time the owners of the nightclub were apprehended in some criminal activities that included drug dealing and accusations of being involved with the mob, all of which further tarnished the reputation of this once-fine hotel. It began to attract drug users, dealers and low-class ladies of the evening, and the hotel staff would be given a cheap room as part of their salaries. Not only visitors to the nightclub but guests and residents of the hotel and apartments would regularly be arrested for various forms of lawbreaking that further led to this establishment's demise.

In its early days, and with the Putnam Hotel's proximity to the Athens Theater, many of the actors, actresses and other people involved with various shows over the years would stay at the Putnam Hotel during the run of the show. At one time, there was even a walkway above ground that led from the back of the hotel to the back of the theater as an easier route for people to take. The hotel would also display a sign in the lobby to let hotel guests know which show was currently playing at the theater, and you could purchase your show tickets from the front desk.

When times were hard, the staff at the Putnam Hotel was often invited to be a part of some of the shows at the theater. They would never be given large parts—just bit parts or playing background parts—but many enjoyed the extra work and one of the chefs at the hotel found his "true calling" while having a bit part in a short running show at the theater. He would also bring food over for the acting company; one year this started out as a three-course meal, but by the end of the running of the show it wound up being franks and beans. This was not the chef's fault. The production company could no longer afford to pay for the wonderful meals as the show was a flop and ticket sales were down. Many of the performers were not happy with the way the meals degraded over the course of the show, but at least it was a free meal.

There are few stories about the Putnam Hotel but all of them have to do with ghosts! It is said that the Putnam Hotel is haunted by the spirits of three people: a married man and woman and another man. Few claim to know how these people became spirits, but all who encounter them have had very similar experiences. The staff has had so many ghostly encounters with one of the spirits on the sixth floor that the hotel has closed that floor off to the public and now uses it strictly for storage. This spirit has been seen as a shadowy figure roaming the halls of the sixth floor. Some see him only out of the corner of their eye, while others see him fully; it is said that he is very frightening to all who encounter him. He also likes to play pranks on the staff, as any respectable poltergeist would or should. It is thought that he may have been residing in the hotel prior to the 1917 fire and may have not gotten out before being consumed by the flames. No bodies were ever found, but one man was missing after the blaze had been put out and no one ever heard from him again. Did he escape the blaze and change his identity? Did he really die in the fire? Was the investigating of the time period so lacking as to not be able to find any remains or was the heat of the fire so intense that it consumed even the smallest remains of this man? Or was he simply killed in the fire and destined to become the poltergeist of the Putnam Hotel? We many never know for sure.

There are, however, countless times when staff has gone to the sixth-floor storage area to retrieve needed items only to find that the door they just unlocked to enter is now locked again. If they lay the keys down for only a moment, the keys move from one end of the room to the other when no one else is in that room. Many of the staff have experienced cold chills as they try to attend to their duties as well as having their hair tugged or touched, and many have reported the smell of smoke or bunt wood all on the sixth floor at all times of the day and night.

A few guests of the Putnam Hotel have ventured up to the sixth floor after hearing the staff speak of the presence that is there, even though they are told it is off-limits to guests. The few that have been brave enough to follow their hearts, and not their heads, have made a hasty retreat from the sixth floor, and others are hard-pressed to get them to talk about their experiences with the pesky poltergeist. One man who was brave enough to ascend the stairway to the sixth floor and even braver to talk about his time spent there stated that when he was at the end of the hall, where the door to the stairway is, he could see the dark shadowy figure of a man standing at the opposite end of the hallway staring at him. He slowly made his way toward the dark figure when he suddenly saw the shadowy man racing toward him with heavy footsteps pounding and echoing through the otherwise empty hall. The next thing he

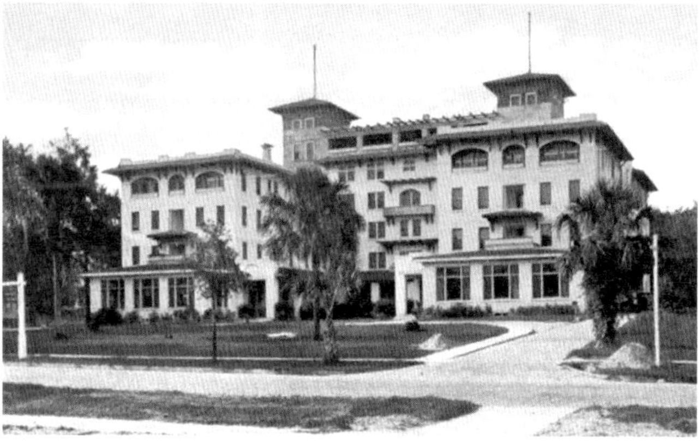

Postcard of the Putnam Hotel in its heyday. *Courtesy of the State of Florida Archives—Florida Memory Project.*

knew he was waking up on the floor with a splitting headache. He quickly went back down to his room on the fourth floor and said he couldn't get the smell of rotting flesh and burnt wood out of his nostrils. His skin was cold to the touch and he was visibly shaken by his experience. He left the hotel that same night and has never stayed at the Putnam Hotel again.

The other ghosts at the Putnam Hotel are not quite as frightening. The story goes that a married couple was renting a small apartment at the hotel during a long-running show at the Athens Theater. The wife was an actress in the show and her husband was a part-time lighting technician. One night, when the show was over, the man caught his wife embracing another man and accepting a bouquet of flowers from him. He waited until they returned to their room on the third floor of the hotel and began to question her loyalties to him. She was enraged and an argument ensued. The couple continued to argue and at one point the woman hit her husband across the face with the bouquet of flowers. His reaction was to smack her across her face and throw her down onto the hardwood floor. She got back to her feet and hit him again and the argument increased in tone and pitch. They kept going until other guests called the front desk to complain. The front desk clerk went to the room and told the couple to keep it down or get out. They agreed to quiet down and bedded down for the night; the man slept in an easy chair while the wife slept in the bed, leaving the dismembered flowers strewn across the floor.

The following day, while the wife was at rehearsals, her husband went to a local pawn shop and purchased a handgun. His intentions were to get the truth out of his wife that very night as soon as she returned to their room. After that night's performance, he waited in their room for her to return. He watched out the window and again saw his wife embracing the other man and accepting yet another bouquet of flowers from him. When she finally arrived at the room, her husband was not there. She didn't know that he had left the room to confront the other man, but the other man was nowhere to be found. When her husband returned to the Putnam Hotel, he decided to block the elevator door so that if anyone came from the front desk on this night he would not be stopped or interrupted until she told him the truth.

When he opened the door to their room, he found that she was already lying in the bed in her night clothes, the bouquet of flowers resting gently on the night table at her side. He roused her from the bed and the argument began again. She professed her innocence and the argument heightened. The man pulled the gun and threatened to kill himself. He felt she no longer loved him and didn't want to live with the thought of her loving another man. His wife tried to reason with him but he was convinced that she was a harlot and was cheating on him. When the wife continued to speak, he covered his ears and began to whistle, still holding the gun in his right hand. She finally went to reach for the gun and it went off, accidentally killing her with one shot through her head. The man was so distraught at seeing his wife's lifeless body lying in a pool of blood on the floor that his guilt lead him to turn the gun on himself and to take his own life as well.

If he would have waited just one more second for an explanation from his wife, he would have discovered that the man she had been embracing and receiving flowers from each night was her brother, whom she hadn't seen since they were in their teens. Her brother had seen her maiden name on a program and was in town on business and decided to come see her in the show each night and visit with her for a few moments before she returned home to the man she truly loved. He always brought her fresh flowers, as he did when they were children when she was feeling ill or just down in the dumps. The innocence that she had professed all along was true and now two people were lying dead in a room on the third floor of the hotel.

The spirits of this couple are still quite active at the Putnam Hotel, though. Each night, about an hour or so after the Athens Theater closes, you can hear a man and a woman arguing throughout the halls of the third floor. Some nights you can also hear two gunshots being fired about one minute apart. You can also hear whistling coming from the center of the hallway on the third floor, just before the first gunshot rings out. The elevator will stop at the third floor, but the door has to be forced open—some say it's because the spirit of the man still blocks the elevator door each night to stop his wife's supposed lover from rescuing her or from the hotel staff from stopping the argument again. Others say they have seen the couple in a certain room on the third floor that they occupied when they were alive. The man is slumped over in the easy chair and the wife is lying face down on the floor in what appears to be a pool of blood. This room always smells of fresh flowers and a cold chill is ever present no matter how high you turn the heater up.

If you decide to stay at the Putnam Hotel, be warned! The musty smell, the dilapidated rooms and the insect infestations are all real. The rattling pipes, brown water and fairly inadequate amenities are also very real. The spirits are just as real and they do not like being disturbed. With regards to the poltergeist on the sixth floor being very possessive about *his* floor, it is best for those still among the living to steer clear of the entire area. There are few cases in the history of paranormal investigating or ghost hunting of a spirit actually causing harm to a living human, but it does happen. This spirit is well documented and may injure you if you offend him in any way or even if you don't. Spirits with this much power and energy have been known to physically injure the living and have no qualms about doing so. After all, what do they have to lose?

If you are lucky enough to get the exact room on the third floor where the married couple perished, you may find yourself having a very restless night. The only time that the staff rents this room is when the rest of the hotel is full. They won't tell you the exact room number if asked, so don't bother. If you are lucky enough to get a room on the third floor, it is well advised to take the stairs up. The elevator will not open on that floor unless you physically force it open with your hands, and this is no easy task. If you are staying on another floor and decide to venture onto the third floor and listen closely in the hallway in the late hours of the night, you may be lucky enough to relive the argument along with the couple, hear the man whistling once again and hear those gunshots piercing the night air.

Some guests of the Putnam Hotel that have stayed in that specific room on the third floor have left in the middle of the night, never to stay at the hotel again. They say the sadness felt on the entire floor is almost overwhelming—the air feels thick and heavy and you can't help but feel empathy for the couple who perished there. Once you turn in for the night and the argument begins, you can hear the muffled voices getting louder and louder. As the argument progresses, the temperature in the room drops severely and cold chills on your body are soon to follow. The smell of fresh flowers is so overpowering that many feel nauseous, and those who have seen the lifeless bodies and the hauntingly evident pool of blood on the floor race from the room still in their nightclothes, never to be heard from again.

References

In addition to the following sources, the Cassadaga Hotel and its staff and the State of Florida Archives assisted in the research for this book.

Cassadaga Spiritualist Camp. http://www.cassadaga.org.

The City of DeLand. http://www.deland.org.

"Civil War Women." http://civilwarwomen.blogspot.com.

Cook, Walter Henry. *Secret Political Societies in the South During the Period of Reconstruction.* Press of Evangelical Publishing House, 1914.

Davis, Susan Lawrence. *Authentic History of the Ku Klux Klan, 1865–1877.* W.G. Mori, 1924.

Edmonds, George. *Facts and Falsehoods Concerning the War on the South 1861–1865.* Whitefish, MT: Kessinger Publishing, 1904.

Florida Office of Cultural & Historical Preservation. Division of Historical Resources. http://www.flheritage.com.

Florida Trail Association. http://www.floridatrail.org/web/index.php.

My Florida Archives. http://www.dhr.dos.state.fl.us.

Owens, Elizabeth. *How to Communicate With Spirits.* Woodbury, MN: Llewellyn Publications, 2001.

Rutherford, Mildred Lewis. *Truths of History.* Whitefish, MT: Kessinger Publishing, 1920.